By the Word of Their Testimony

"And they overcame him because of the blood of the Lamb and because of the ***word of their testimony****..."*
Revelation 12:11

Take Up Your Cross and Follow Me

Book 4

NarrowRoad Publishing House

By the Word of Their Testimony
"Take Up Your Cross and Follow Me"

Published by:
NarrowRoad Publishing House
POB 830
Ozark, MO 65721 U.S.A.

The materials from Restore Ministries were written for the sole purpose of encouraging women. For more information, please take a moment to visit us at:

EncouragingWomen.org

RestsoreMinistries.net

Unless otherwise indicated, most Scripture verses are taken from the *New American Standard Bible* (NASB). Scripture quotations marked KJV are taken from the *King James Version* of the Bible, and Scripture quotations marked NIV are taken from the *New International Version.* Our ministry is not partial to any particular version of the Bible but **loves** them all so that we are able to help every woman in any denomination who needs encouragement and who has a desire to gain greater intimacy with her Savior.

Library of Congress Control number: 2017902470

ISBN: 1-931800-36-7
ISBN 13: 978-1-931800-36-5

Contents

Introduction

Your Divine Appointment

"I was **crying** to the LORD with my voice,
And He **answered me** from His holy mountain"
Psalm 3:4.

Have you been searching for marriage help? It's not by chance, nor is it by coincidence, that you are reading this booklet. God has heard your cry for help in your marriage dilemma. He predestined this DIVINE APPOINTMENT to give you the hope that you so desperately need right now!

If you have been told that your marriage is hopeless or that without your spouse's help your marriage cannot be restored, then this is the book you need. Read this over and over so you will begin to believe that God is MORE than able to restore ANY marriage, including YOURS!

For ALL the testimonies of those who once had "seemingly" hopeless marriages that are now restored, go to our website – RestoreMinistries.net to read those that we have received since the printing of this book that we post on our website.

We know and understand what you are going through since WE, and MANY others who have come to our ministry for help, have a restored marriage and family! No matter what others have told you, your marriage is NOT hopeless!! We KNOW, after twelve years of ministry, that God is able to restore ANY marriage, even YOURS!

If you have been crying out to God for more help, someone who understands, someone you can talk to, then join our Internet Restoration Fellowship OnLine and receive an ePartner (email partner) who will help you see your marriage through to restoration. Since beginning this fellowship, we have seen more marriages restored on a regular basis than we ever thought possible!

So, if you are really serious in your desire to restore your marriage, then our fellowship is the answer. For more information or to join, go to our website. We would love for you to be a part of our Restoration Fellowship!

Who are we and what are we hoping to do?

Restore Ministries helps those who have found themselves in a hopeless situation: women whose spouse is in adultery, has left her, has filed for divorce, or any other seemingly impossible marital situation. They have often sought help, but everyone (many times even their pastors) has told them it was hopeless. We believe that no marriage is hopeless – regardless of the circumstances. We offer hope, help and encouragement through our website, our Restoration Fellowship, and a variety of resources.

In 2001, Restoration Fellowship was birthed to minister more effectively to the needs of those seriously seeking restoration. Within a year the fellowship grew to over 400 committed members and increases daily with members from all over the world.

Restore Ministries has never sought advertising or paid for placement in search engines but has instead grown by word of mouth. Though often ostracized by the established church, because of those who have cried out to God for help when their own church, pastor, family and friends offered them no hope or support, it has given hope and has been the oasis in the desert for the desperate, the hurting, the rejected.

Often accused of being extreme, radical, out-of-balance or legalistic, the message in all our resources is founded firmly on the Word of God, encouraging those seeking restoration to live the message that Jesus proclaimed, beginning with the familiar Beatitudes.

RMI teaches the good news of God's Word to bring healing to the brokenhearted, comfort to those in pain, and freedom to prisoners of despondency and sin through the truth of His Word, giving them the hope that is "against all hope" through the Power of Jesus Christ, the Mighty Counselor and Good Shepherd.

Our site and our resources minister to the hurting all over the world with the intent of creating a deeper and more intimate walk with the Lord that results in the hurting healed, the bound freed, the naked clothed, the lost saved and broken marriages restored. We minister to women from more than 15 countries including Switzerland, Hong Kong, New Zealand, Sweden, Philippines, Brazil and Germany, with large followings in Australia, Canada, and Africa. Our books have been translated into Spanish, Portuguese, Tagalog (Filipino), Afrikaans, and French.

Jesus said that you "will know them by their fruits." This book *By the Word of Their Testimony* is filled with testimonies of hopeless marriages that were restored, marriages that give glory to God and to the Power of His Word. This book grows at such a phenomenal rate that we are unable to keep up with reprinting due to the number of testimonies that pour into their office. If you have any doubt about the validly of our ministry, you won't after reading this awesome book. It will show you not only hopeless marriages that were restored, but more importantly, it will show you men and women who have been completely transformed into God-lovers and are now committed on-fire Christians, many of whom were saved through this ministry.

Below is a small sampling of the letters of gratitude that Restore Ministries has received. Please note when you read the letters that they give all the praise and glory to the Lord. This ministry was founded and continues to grow on the premise that "if He be lifted up, He will draw all men to Himself" and "the Lord will share His glory with no man."

"Let Another Praise You" Proverbs 27:2

I want to thank this ministry for all the support they are giving me and my RJ. I am finding I am not so focused on my Marriage as I am with doing the will of My Lord. This ministry has been pivotal in my journey and my walk with Christ. I am so grateful that I was able to find some where that would give me the resources to find my place with My Lord. I just want another woman to feel the joy and the peace that I have had with this ministry.

I was at the end of my rope, I did not care if I lived or died as my life was so changed by my EH walking out on me. This ministry saved my life. If it does anything at all it pointed me in the right direction to My Lord. It helped me see that it was my relationship with him that mattered. No human Man can give you what My Lord can give you, No human Man can fill your heart the way My Lord can. It is important for all areas of your life to know that He is here and he will always be here.

~ Laurie in Canada
THANK You!! I am currently on my own restoration journey for my marriage and this is the most incredible journey. I have learned so many different things about myself and what God is doing and has been doing for me. I have grown up in a time that seemed simple and right yet when my life came crashing down around me I struggled. Nearly one year later I found a RYM book (and I will never know how the information ended up in my hands) and I truly believe it was God who led me to your ministry. My life has changed completely. God is wonderful. He is providing for me each and every single day.

When I found RMI I had been separated for approximately a year. I was pursuing and was contentious. Wow, how things have changed and how much I love the changes! I have a calmness now knowing that God is in control of my life.

Thank you so very much for everything. God has used you to help change me. Thank you for being one of God's prophets and for what you are doing for me.

~ Laurie in Florida

Thank You to everyone at RMI. Your online courses have helped me to see all I had done in the break down of my marriage. and what I need to do to correct my short comming and become the knid of wife the Lord wanted me to be. I tell every women I come into contact with that is having marriage problems about the RYM book and your ministry, it has been a Godsend for me as I work toward knowing the Lord as my Husband. And also to your partners.

My husband just packed everything up and left one day while I was at work, leaving the state. I did'nt hear from him for 6 months. I was so fillied with hurt, anger and pain. I wanted my husband and my marriage I did'nt understand what was so bad that he felt he had to do what he did the way he did it. It was that pain that lead me to the internet looking for help on restoring my marriage. Again, I would like to thank all of you. I will give your books to hurting women I come accross in need but I also try to get some in our local library.

Thank You again for the books!!

~ Alisa in Florida

We put this book together because we believe that as you spend some time reading these incredible and awesome testimonies of seemingly hopeless marriages that were miraculously restored, you will be encouraged and know without a doubt...

NOTHING IS IMPOSSIBLE WITH GOD!!

Nothing is Impossible with God!

"Looking at them, Jesus said,
'With people it is impossible,
but not with God;
for all things are possible with God.'"
—Mark 10:27

"And they overcame him because of the blood of the Lamb and because of the **word of THEIR testimony**, and they did not love their life even to death." Revelation 12:11.

The following testimonies are filled with miracles of men and women who took God at His Word and believed that "nothing was impossible with God!" Those who have had the miracle of a restored marriage have several things in common. All "delighted themselves in the Lord" and He gave them "the desires of their heart." All of them "hoped against hope" when their situation seemed hopeless.

All of them "fought the good fight" and "finished their course." All of them were determined "not to be overcome with evil" but instead to "overcome evil with good." All were willing to "bless their enemies" and to pray for them that "despitefully used and persecuted them." All "turned the other cheek" and "walked the extra mile." All realized that it was "God who removed lover and friend far from" them and it was God who "made them a loathing" to their spouse. All of them understood and believed that it is NOT the will of man (or woman) but the "will of God" who would "turn the heart" whichever way He chose.

All refused to fight in "the flesh" but chose to battle "in the spirit." None were concerned to protect themselves, but trusted themselves "to Him who judges righteously." All of their trust was "in the Lord" because their trust was "the Lord." All released their attorneys (if that was part of their testing) since they "would rather be wronged or defrauded." All of them "got out of the way of wickedness" and "let the unbeliever leave" since they "were called to peace." All refused to do "evil for evil or insult for insult." All loved their spouse who may have been unfaithful because they knew that "love never fails."

This is the same journey that the Lord took me on back in 1989. That year I made a promise to God that if He would restore my marriage to my husband, I would devote my life to telling others about Him and His desire and ability to restore ANY marriage no matter what the circumstances. The Lord was faithful and restored my marriage, suddenly, two years later after a divorce. (Yes! AFTER a divorce!) Now I faithfully, with the Lord's continued help, love, support, and guidance, spread the GOOD news that nothing—NOT A THING—is impossible with God!

It is important to know that our ministry was FOUNDED to help all those who were told by pastors and Christian friends that their situations were HOPELESS. Those who come to us for hope are facing a spouse who is deep in adultery, who has moved out (often in with the other person), who has already filed for divorce or whose divorce has gone through. 99% of those who come, come alone for help since their spouse is not interested in saving their marriage, but is desperately trying to get out. Over 95% claim that they are Christians and most are married to Christians. Over half are in some type of Christian service and many of the men who are involved with other woman are pastors who have left not only their wife and children, but their church as well.

If you, or if someone you know, is facing devastation in their marriage, there is hope. Read these awesome testimonies that prove that God is MORE than able to restore ANY marriage!

Chapter 1

Janie

"Oh Lord, You took up my case;
You redeemed my life"
—Lamentations 3:58

"Pressing On"

"Come and listen, all you who fear God; let me tell you what he has done for me. I cried out to him with my mouth; his praise was on my tongue. If I had cherished sin in my heart, the Lord would not have listened; but God has surely listened and heard my voice in prayer. Praise be to God who has not rejected my prayer or withheld his love from me!" (Psalm 66: 16-20, NIV).

Dear sister, I truly am "the least of all these" and yet GOD saw fit to forgive me and give me another chance! After a series of marriages in my youth, I turned to JESUS as my Savior, finally making HIM the LORD of my life and stayed alone (but not alone!) for almost 15 years. In many ways this was the best 15 years of my life, I used to tell HIM and others "my life is almost perfect!"

Meanwhile, I felt HIM talking to me about a new relationship. Although I resisted at first in the flesh, in time HE did bring it, and my husband and I met at a bible study. Because of my past, I asked the LORD for extraordinary confirmation and HE brought minis people from another country to our church. They prophesied over us "GOD brought you together for a ministry" and follow-up confirmation.

So I trusted GOD and said Yes. My children's father has been dead many years and I did encourage my husband to try "everything he could" to be restore with the mother of his children, though never married, who had left him for OM (his first wife had died). He did ask her about this on more than one occasion, over several months, but she would have none of it. So trusting GOD, we were married. Almost immediately after our wedding, (a few days into the honeymoon) the enemy began working to destroy "the plans" our GOD had for us.

It was very painful as my husband still had very deep hurts, trauma and fears from his whole life. At this time he had been back in church for about three years. He told everyone that he had prayed for a Christian wife and had "got one in spades!" and would laugh. He wasn't prepared for how GOD answered that prayer though. That was the good part. However, I did NOT know how to deal with all of this and though, rarely "returned evil for evil" I reacted to everything wrong, protesting and asking questions. I was the Christian wife that my husband prayed for, but I had a LOT to learn and much of my own healing! I also would attempt to lead and teach (when he asked me,) and go to church without him—WRONG! (As I later found out through RMI.) Anyway, the crisis peaked and soon he wanted a divorce.

However, GOD was good enough to warn me the day before. I was driving to a "prayers for the nation" meeting with the ladies intercessory group when we stopped chatting and our leader said that GOD told her I was with them so they could pray for me. She lead us in 2 Corinthians 10:4 (casting down imaginations and every high thing that exalts itself against the knowledge of GOD and taking my husbands' every thought captive" she did not even know about our situation!) After the prayer meeting, she prophesied that my husband would come back to the LORD and serve HIM and right then another lady gave me the Restore Ministries website! I was so grateful to GOD that HE had heard my cries and would speak to me this way that I immediately started fasting that night and told HIM I would "fast for as long as it took." Also that night, I read the Restore pages enough to know what to do and not do the next day, and ordered the materials. "Therefore also now, says the Lord, turn and keep on coming to Me with all your heart, with fasting, with weeping, and with mourning [until every hindrance is removed and the broken fellowship is restored]" Joel 2:12 (AMB).

The next afternoon my husband said "I'm filing for divorce tomorrow." Beloved, I was already prepared!! When he asked me for a response, I said, "Well, that's not what I want but I won't stand in your way," along with staying "quiet and gentle." He did keep the lawyer appointment the next day (a Friday) and came home quiet. I confess I was "hiding out" from the sheriff (d-papers) all weekend, as my husband stayed away for most of it. Then on Sunday, he told me that he had not gone through with it, that "it just didn't feel right!" I just agreed. He also spoke softly a profound truth: "Wow, GOD sure can change hearts" in an almost whimsical manner. I should have just believed at that point, but I also confess that I checked our bank balance online and saw the check to the lawyer for $3500. After he told me he cancelled it, I continued fasting and staying in the "quiet and gentle spirit" and so on from what I had learned from RMI by that time but unfortunately, still kept checking the balance and it was not refunded.

I was really stressing this, but continued the extended fast while crying out to the LORD alone, and reading the Word and Restore materials. I checked one last time (11 days after the fast began), which was a Monday and still no returned check. My husband came back from town and we were sitting on the sofa holding hands (GOD was already honoring my obedience!). I just listened to him talk but prayed inside "LORD, I am about to jump out of my skin!" and other such pleas. How can I find out about the lawyer without questioning my husband? (I didn't want him to FEEL doubted) Please give me YOUR question for him." So, the LORD had me ask him, "So, Honey, how are things today?" My husband responded, "Well, I went this morning and got my money back from the lawyer if that says anything." I just nodded and smiled and inside was SHOUTING TO THE LORD!! "Blessed are the people of whom this is true; blessed are the people whose GOD is the LORD!" (Psalm 144: 15)

The *Restore your Marriage* book and *Facing Divorce* helped me see what the enemy was up to, how I had sinned and how to "fight in the spirit." I am just starting to delve farther into *A Wise Woman*, wow, what an excellent resource for all women! Everything I have read, seen and heard has helped me, RMI, GOD has woven your materials together as a beautiful tapestry!

GOD has finally gotten through to me that HE wants me to just trust HIM, a Word that HE had given me at a prophesy service two years before, HE taught me that HE is listening (as evidenced by the prayers from my Sisters in the car that day and many other ways) and that HE has much for me to learn, as I found out from this precious ministry. GOD is showing me that HE is faithful and can be trusted, even when "the will of man" is contrary to my prayers. I wish I could say that I fully trust HIM now, as I should. So I continue to pray that HE "will complete the work" HE has started in me, for HIS glory! Also, I DO THANK HIM for this trial as GOD has brought me to FULL repentance before HIM for all the sins of my past (which are "ever before me") and I thank HIM for HIS great Mercy! Before this trial I had not really done this, as I should. I believe HE needed me to do this before HE could really use me in HIS ministry and used this current spiritual crisis to bring me to my knees.

GOD really used the Restore principles to change me. "The teaching of the wise is a fountain of life, turning a man from the snares of death" (Proverbs 13:14 NIV); "Let others praise you", Erin! I thought I was "ok" because I was not returning evil. But GOD used you to show me that this was just a minimum effort! This is the world's minimum standard, and I had bought it "hook, line, and sinker" and it nearly sunk my marriage! I have learned that I must be quiet and gentle instead of reacting (something I still struggle with when the enemy catches me 'off-guard'), wait for my husband to lead, and to cry out to "HIM alone" when I'm hurting and also to ask HIM for every need I have. PRAISE GOD FOR HIS FAITHFULNESS!

Now when my husband asks me about a biblical principle, I just smile and shrug. If he presses, I may say for example: "Charles Stanley says this or Joyce Meyer (he loves her!) says that, but what do you think?" The day when my precious husband will teach me from the Word of GOD is something I long for too! Another thing I have learned is that my protesting was the same as complaining! "Do everything without complaining or arguing" (Philippians 2:14 NIV). Also, I now usually ask GOD when I need or even want something and you know what?! HE brings it, often through my husband! Even a beautiful birthday present six months "late" when I did not complain to my husband about no gift or card! LISTEN—GOD HEARS YOU AND CARES—so don't talk to anyone else, speak to Him about all your needs!!

I have also learned to bind scriptures to myself and my husband (i.e. casting down imaginations from BOTH of us). GOD has also led me do a really sweet thing in speaking Judges 6:12b to my husband when he leaves the house: "The LORD is with you mighty warrior." He loves it! To GOD be the glory!!

And last "but not least" I repented before a small group church family for the things I had "uncovered" and asked them to believe with me for restoration. I no longer share with them any more about my husband. I'm sure there are many more things GOD taught me from RMI and from HIS word and I pray HE will continue to teach me for the rest of my life.

Although the divorce was cancelled, things did not start to get better for quite a while! But with GOD'S help, I continued fasting, praying, and applying the principles and seeking GOD and HIS Word. Sometimes I wanted to "bail out" but HE would bring scriptures to my mind and heart just in time! The story of Jehoshaphat got me on my face in worship, and other times, standing to praise HIM, BEFORE the victory (2 Chronicles 20:15-24). This is where an enemy much too strong for King Jehoshaphat to triumph over was coming to conquer the villages and it was prophesied to him "Do not be afraid or discouraged because of this vast army. For the battle is not yours, but God's." Then Jehoshaphat took his BATTLE POSITION on his face before the LORD and he and many in Judah and Jerusalem "fell down in worship" while some "stood up and praised the LORD." (The LORD had told me years before that HALLELUJAH is our battle cry!) Then, they gave THANKS to the LORD and proclaimed, "His love endures forever."

When they did this, "the LORD set ambushes" against the enemy and they turned on themselves. When everyone looked, all in the enemy camp were dead. Beloved, ALL they had to do was acknowledge that "the battle is the LORD'S," get on their faces in worship, stand on their feet in praise and thank HIM! The LORD did ALL the rest! HALLELUJAH TO THE LIVING GOD!!

Other scriptures I hung on to:

Psalms! (Erin is so right about these!) My favorites are: Psalms 9:1, 9-10; 27:13-14; 32:7-8; 33:4-11; 35:22; 100:1-5; 138:3, 6-8; 143:8-10; 144:7-8,15; 146:2 and 150. Also Proverbs, 9:7; 12:15-16; 13:3, 10; 14:1, 12, 15, 27; 15:1, 31; 16:2, 9, 24; 17:9, 22, 28; 18:10, 12, 21; 19:11, 21; 20:22, 24; 21:1-3, 30; 22:9, 11, 17-19; 23:18, 26; 24:3-4, 17-18, 29; 25:21-22; 26:11; 27:17; 28:13; and of course, 31:10-31. Look them up, copy them, mark your Bible and renew your mind with them.

Others verses He gave to me:

Whenever I began to grow tired of constantly following the principles (yes, I did): "And let us not be weary in well doing: for in due season we shall reap, if we faint not." (Galatians 6:9 KJV)

Whenever the enemy tried to trap me in fear: "For I am the LORD your GOD, who takes hold of your right hand and says to you, Do not fear; I will help you." (Isaiah 41:13 NIV) "You are my hiding place; you will protect me from trouble and surround me with songs of deliverance (Psalm 332: 7 NIV).

And, when in the fire (Daniel 3: 16-18) We must NOT bow to fear!

This one came to me when I had no hope at all in the natural: "Be glad for all God is planning for you. Be patient in trouble, and always be prayerful. (Romans 12:12 NLT)

When I became willing to accept whatever GOD wanted: "I am still confident of this: I will see the goodness of the LORD in the land of the living. Wait for the LORD; be strong and take heart and wait for the LORD." (Psalm 27: 13-14 NIV)

This one helped me stay when I wanted to bolt: " So don't throw it all away now. You were sure of yourselves then. It's still a sure thing! But you need to stick it out, staying with God's Plan so you'll be there for the promised completion. It won't be long now, He's on the way: He'll show up most any minute. But anyone who is right with me thrives on loyal trust; if he cuts and runs, I won't be very happy." (Hebrews 10: 35-38 The Message Bible)

And then, when I was questioning that I hadn't heard GOD correctly, that all the prophecies had been wrong, HE gave me a word: "GOD wants you to know that HE is proud of you, of the stand you have taken, HE sees every effort you make, no matter how small and HE takes note of it. HE says you WILL reap a harvest if you faint not."

At every turn, there were promises from HIM, some from the Word, and some from RMI praise reports. Once, as I prayed about whether GOD wanted me to keep a lawyer appointment (that my Pastor had advised, just for my "protection", though he would have admonished me for initiating a divorce) I asked GOD for a sign if HE did not want me to keep it. I opened up the RMI website and clicked on praise reports: It was a praise report that I had sent in a couple of weeks before! I said, "Ok GOD, I get it!" I called at once and cancelled. THANK YOU JESUS!

One morning right before my breakthrough, the LORD also gave me a picture of the Passover, where the Israelites painted their doorsteps with blood so the LORD would recognize HIS own and "Passover" their houses with the destruction HE was bringing. Remember the LORD told the Israelites to paint their doorposts with the blood of a lamb to be a sign to pass over the houses of the faithful? Exodus 12:13 says "The blood will be a sign for you on the houses where you are; and when I see the blood, I will pass over you. No destructive plague will touch you when I strike Egypt."

Then, of course, our LORD sacrificed HIMSELF as the ULTIMATE LAMB! First Corinthians 5:7b says "For Christ, our Passover Lamb has been sacrificed." First Peter 1:19 says "But with the precious blood of Christ, a lamb without blemish or defect." I have learned that anointing oil (oil blessed and prayed over) that we use to pray for the sick, etc. represents the blood of JESUS. So the next thing HE showed me was to anoint my doorpost with oil (representing the Blood) and pray for the destruction of divorce to pass over our home. This was soon after I had "given up" in the flesh (see below).

There have honestly been many "turning points" in this journey. Most I mentioned, like scriptures, along with learning the RMI principles all helped me to "turn." It wasn't until I really of gave up (inside) on my marriage at some point and wanted it to be just us, the Lord and me again, while I continued to fast and pray, but for other people's marriages and not mine. That's when I began to see the "turning" in my husband. While I was busy praying for my Sisters' marriages, GOD was busy at work in mine!

I wish I could say that our restoration was "sudden and complete" but even after restoration it continues to be a difficult process. However, when I read Erin's description, just now, that "if your spouse is home and OW or OM is out of the picture then you are restored" and "when the enemy will come against you even stronger" is when I decided to submit my testimony out of obedience. I can also say honestly and without reservation that GOD HIMSELF has answered my prayers that I He gave me long ago. HOW I PRAISE HIS HOLY NAME! I do greatly miss the "fellowship of believers" but I know GOD will lead my husband to a church of HIS choosing since I let go of my church. Thank You Lord! So you see that GOD loves and cares for even "the least of these" HIS children and being "no respecter of persons" HE will restore your marriage too. "Be cheerfully expectant. Don't quit in hard times; pray all the harder" (Romans 12:12 MSB).

GOD is so faithful Sisters and Brothers! All the things that I had given up hope on, GOD is doing them now! I believe that HE will continue to finish what HE has started in me (and my husband). GOD has a plan and purpose (beyond us) for each of our marriages and HE will have HIS way with all of us! HE IS FAITHFUL!!

THIS IS ALL GOD!! EVERY GOOD THING THAT HAS HAPPENED IS FROM HIM! (James 1:17). Thank YOU LORD JESUS and thank you RMI! No one but our GOD could have fashioned this Awesome Ministry!

And now, without confidence in the flesh I am pressing on toward the goal!

~ Janie in Colorado, Former Fellowship Member, Gratefully RESTORED!

Chapter 2

Marie and Vicki

"The reward of humility and
the fear of the Lord
are riches, honor and life"

—Proverbs 22:4

"Friends' Marriages BOTH Restored!!"

Two women, Marie and Vicki, met by Divine appointment at church one morning. While talking briefly, they found that both of their marriages were in major trouble. They exchanged phone numbers, and, thus, God answered each of their prayers for "someone to help them." Both of them wanted their marriages, yet each of their husbands were trying to get out of their commitment. Both ladies were newly saved and both of their husbands would have nothing to do with church.

These friends began going to a Wednesday night home group together. One evening a couple whose marriage had been restored through Restore Ministries just happened to visit this home group. Each woman shared her prayer request for marital help. One of the husbands was still at home but sleeping in another room and hadn't spoken to his wife for almost four months. As the other woman began to share her request, she broke down weeping. Her husband was going to court in less than two weeks; he was divorcing her.

The restored couple just looked at one another and squeezed each other's hands. They knew why the Lord had Providentially led them across town for the meeting that night. When they broke for prayer, the restored couple walked over to the woman whose husband was divorcing her and asked if they might pray for her. They shared that they had a restored marriage, that the Lord had obviously sent them there that night, and that God was going to turn the whole situation around. They finished by stating, "God won't allow the divorce to go through." As they spoke, tears ran down her face and dripped onto the floor. After they prayed, the three of them went over to the other woman to pray for her.

After prayer that night, all four of them sat on the couch visiting while the couple shared their entire testimony of how God restored their marriage. The entire home group listened in. Then the husband excused himself and went to the trunk of their car. He returned with two books and handed each of the women a *Restore Your Marriage* book.

More than a month had passed when the restored couple ran into the group leader of that home group and inquired about these two young women. He stated quite calmly that they were doing well and both of them were now attending church with their husbands! After recovering from the shock, the couple asked for details.

It seems that the husband of the woman who hadn't spoken to her in four months, unexpectedly accepted an invitation to go to a potluck dinner at her home group when the leader called and got him on the phone! His wife, of course, was ecstatic when he told her. But when she called for directions it wasn't that night! The group leader told her he had misunderstood; it wasn't that night, but next week! Her heart sank. Then he proceeded to tell her to just "come on over anyway."

The couple did go and spent the evening just visiting with the group leader and his family. After the meal the group leader asked her husband if he wanted to take a little walk while the ladies cleaned up. While they were walking, the group leader said to her husband, "Son, the problems that you and your wife are having, well, everybody has them. You just have to work through the problems." That is just what her husband needed to hear. That night things totally turned around for her and her husband.

For the other woman and her husband it was even more miraculous! Two weeks after she met the restored couple, she went to the courthouse for the divorce hearing. She had released her attorney, as the restored couple had told her that she had to, but because it was so close to the hearing, she was required to go to the hearing or be held in contempt of court.

The young woman sat nervously praying while she waited for their case to be called. She remembered the night the restored couple had prayed and what they had said: "God won't allow the divorce to go through." But here she was about to be called into court. Finally, as she heard their name called she leaped out of her chair. She trembled as she went into the judge's chambers and sat down. Her husband's attorney was there glaring at her. Her head felt like it was spinning as the attorney and judge spoke. Then she heard it: "Divorce granted"!! It felt like a knife pierced through her chest. But then, as the judge leaned over to write his name on the papers, he stopped. He said that his name was not on the papers and that he could NOT GRANT THEM THE DIVORCE!

This woman thought she was dreaming. Had he said what she thought he said? All three of them got up and walked out. This woman's husband and his attorney stood together talking while she leaned against the wall still in shock at what had just happened. The attorney told her husband that he would have to start all over by filing again. Extremely upset, her husband rushed over and grabbed her hand and stomped out.

Two nights later the same group leader called and invited her husband to their home group meeting that night. He accepted!! That evening in the kitchen her husband told the group leader what had transpired two days earlier. He responded by saying, "You know, God hates divorce. And what you experienced was the hand of God stopping you, son. Do you know His Son, Jesus Christ?" Her husband later said that he experienced "**the fear of the Lord**" that night — he got saved right there and then! Nothing is impossible with God. That means NOT A THING!

So if your situation seems hopeless, the Lord has a plan. He is never late. If your divorce is still headed for court, don't despair; instead trust Him, believe Him. If we trust Him, cease striving, wait for Him, and hope against hope, then all things will work together for our good, if we love Him and are called according to His purpose, not our own!

~ *Marie and Vicki in Florida, both RESTORED*

Chapter 3

Samantha

"From every nation, tribe,
people and language,
standing before the throne
and before the Lamb."
—Revelation 7:9

"Mum and Daughter's Marriages BOTH Restored!!"

A young woman wrote to us from Africa requesting help for her marriage. She also shared that her mother ("mum") had already filed for divorce against her father. The rate of exchange is so high in Africa that a *How God Will Restore Your Marriage* book would cost five times what it cost here, not including the shipping charges that were ten times the cost of the book! The Lord led us to send her two books as a gift: one for her and one for her "mum." Within a month we received a praise report that her mother had dropped the divorce and her parents' marriage was restored. Hallelujah!!

Then she went on to say that right after she first wrote to us for help, her marriage took a major turn for the worse — her husband filed for divorce! But PRAISE THE LORD - he suddenly dropped the divorce and now is home!! To God be the glory for the great things He has done!

This testimony has sparked a large following in Africa. God is moving all over the world!!! Right now we have translators working to translate the *Restore Your Marriage* into Afrikaans! This proves it is a "God thing"!

~ Julie and her mum in Nigeria, both RESTORED

"We Aren't Fighting Anymore!"

Samantha sent us a short email to tell us that she thought she had a wonderful marriage, until her husband confessed to her a major sin that he had been hiding. It was then that everything started to fall apart. They fought continuously. Eventually her husband backslid and became suicidal.

Then she ordered the book *How God Will Restore Your Marriage*. She began reading the pages earnestly and faithfully keeping the "Personal Commitments" that she signed in the back of each chapter. She then purchased the workbook for women and did all the homework pages. She also increased her prayer life and found one friend to confess her faults to and pray with.

Just today she wrote that she has a NEW marriage!!! Even her children noticed that "Mom and Dad aren't fighting anymore"! She has just ordered 10 more books. She said, "I know so many women who need this message!"

~ Samantha in Oregon, RESTORED

"OW TOTALLY Out of the Picture!"

A woman with a "quiver full" of children wrote to us. She was in a very painful situation. Her husband was committing adultery with a woman whom this woman worked with. One night her husband and the other woman came into where she worked, sat passionately together and even kissed right in front of her!
The fire was turned up when her husband, who couldn't find an apartment for himself and his adulterous woman, asked her to pack and leave with all their children. His wife had become so weary, she thought it might be "for the best." But the Lord faithfully revealed the truth to her in time. When she realized that this was surely a trap and scheme of the enemy, she prayed to be able to stay. That night her husband came home and said that he didn't want her to go.

Within a week's time, we received word that her husband is now home and the other woman is totally out of the picture! She also said that when she went into the bedroom she saw the Men's Manual lying open on his side of the bed!! She had NO idea where he got it. She also said, "My husband is not even a reader!" Praise the Lord for His faithfulness!!

~ Cindi in Pennsylvania, RESTORED

Chapter 4

Laura

"The refining pot is for silver
and the furnace for gold,
but the Lord tests hearts"

—Proverbs 17:3

"Tests and Trials"

Just 3 months ago I came to Restore Ministries and two weeks later joined the Restoration Fellowship after knowing I needed to let go of my church so I could learn to know Him better.

After visiting the website and reading the testimonies of marriages that had been restored, I was so impressed so I had to order all your books. Wow - did your materials, which are based on God's will for our lives, ever open my eyes!!! I had always looked at my husband's sins, but never my own until after reading your books and then I got to work putting myself into God's Word the Bible! What a comfort to realize I wasn't alone in what I was going through.

When my husband called me two days after my birthday the first thing he said is, "Boy are you changing and repenting!" My husband asked me at that time if he could come home and take me out for my birthday, which I of course, agreed to! He came home immediately and we spent four days together and at the end he asked if we could get back together again!

There were so MANY tests when my husband was gone and many more after he returned (so I am so glad for the time I had to learn what to do and how to focus on the Lord, my Husband), but I did everything as all your books taught me. When He asked me what I expected out of this relationship I now knew what I should say. My response was to be able to love him as a wife should love her husband, and to respect and honor him until death do us part. He laughed and squeezed me tight!!!

~ Cheryl in Maine, Fellowship Member, RESTORED

"God Moved Suddenly!"

First, I just want to say Praise God! He is so faithful to His promises!! My story is like so many others. I was devastated when my husband called after work one day and said he wasn't coming home. I knew that our marriage wasn't great, but I never dreamed that things would go that far. I later found out that my husband had been unfaithful.

It was after he had been gone a week that someone recommended Restore Ministries to me. I cried and cried as I read the opening page of the website. Finally, some hope! I ordered the book, workbook and joined the fellowship right away after letting go of my church (that told me things contrary to what I began learning). I was shocked at how much I didn't know about what God and His Word had to say about marriage, divorce, and separation and how the Lord would be my Husband. But after reading the material, I knew that God would restore my marriage, not me or anyone else.

I began applying the principles right away. Although I didn't see immediate changes in my husband in how he treated me, I felt peace like I had not felt in years. After my husband had been gone about three weeks, I re-dedicated my life to the Lord, became His bride, and for what I believe is the first time in my life, I actually had assurance of my salvation. What a gift!!! Thank you RMI!!

Then suddenly one morning after my husband had been gone for almost two months, I got my miracle phone call!! Just the day before I had told God not to bother, I didn't want restoration, I just really wanted my new Husband. Yet the next day my husband called me from work and told me that his living arrangements were changing. I just said "ok" because I no longer cared. He then began to weep and told me that he missed his family, his home, and his life. He wanted to try to get it all back.

Wow God is so amazing!! Just at the point that He became all I wanted, God restored.

It was only 10 days earlier that my husband had been talking about how we were going to divide up our household items, about child visitation, and about how I needed to figure out a way to support myself!!! God moved so suddenly! That Sunday he asked me to join him and we went to church and during the song service and the invitation, he sat in his seat with his eyes closed and tears were streaming down his face!!! He found his salvation just like I had been assured of mine!!

~ *Laura in Tennessee, Fellowship Member, RESTORED*

"Restored - To Him Be All the Glory!"

After praying and fasting for six years, I asked the Holy Spirit to guide me through the Internet to some ministry that would help me. The Holy Spirit guided me to Restore Ministries, wow! I couldn't wait to order the books, ordered and watched the videos one after another and then repeated them. Next I let go of my church and joined your fellowship! As soon as I received the books, I read and reread them, marked them and read them some more. It has truly been a tremendous blessing in my life, as well as the lives of others whom I've shared more books after buying a dozen!

After applying the principles in your books as well as the hedge of thorns, within three weeks my husband came home one day shaking in his boots, and with tears in his eyes running down his face. All I can say is, DON'T GIVE UP! I believe that what helped me the most was to be obedient to God's Word in everything, once I learned the truth. That's what really did it!

God bless you, Erin! God's blessings to you, your ministry, and your beautiful family!

~ *Marsha in North Dakota, Fellowship Member, RESTORED*

Chapter 5

Jim

"... for we walk by faith,
not by sight!"
—2 Corinthians 5:7

"Celebrating 20 Years!"

We recently received a letter from a man, Jim, in Texas who reported that after 15 months of separation, his wife of over twenty years has RETURNED HOME — praise the Lord!!!! She had filed for divorce in May, about two months after he received both of our books for men. The Lord led him to apologize for all of his wrongdoing in their marriage. However, she seemed unimpressed and still was determined to divorce him.

Then in September, his wife found herself in a very serious situation. Jim asked if there was anything he could do something to help her. To his surprise, she accepted his offer for help! Instantly, his wife's opinion of him changed and she decided to move back home and recommit to their marriage!!! She is NOW home—where they celebrated their 20th Wedding Anniversary!!!!

~ Jim in Texas, RESTORED

Note: So often men and women panic when they don't have regular contact with their spouses since the Lord has "changed them." God always makes a way to reunite spouses. He often allows a crisis in a spouse's life as an answer to our prayers, but ONLY when we obey and leave room for HIM to move!!

"Husband Packed Bags—Came Home!"

A young woman, Michelle, had two small boys, when she found out that her husband had not just left her, but was actually living with another woman who had recently had his baby. Michelle was devastated, but she sought the Lord for help. Soon after, she met a couple in her church who told her that they had a restored marriage, introduced her to Restore Ministries resources, and said that they would help her.

Michelle began meeting regularly with this couple to pray. Soon after reading *How God can and will Restore your Marriage* and began to meet with the older woman to study *A Wise Woman*. She then felt led to begin to apply the principles on fasting with prayer. However, things got much worse the more she prayed and fasted. One day as she answered her door, she was shocked as a sheriff served her with divorce papers. Instead of falling apart, she took the papers in hand and headed to the older couple's house to pray. The three of them held hands and prayed together against the divorce papers.

At that exact hour in another state, her husband was packing his bags. As he headed south and came to a fork in the road, he asked God to steer his truck, to the right would be home, to the left would be to join the other woman. His wife's prayers were answered — the truck pulled abruptly to the RIGHT!

Once her husband was home, she shared with her husband about her prayers, fasting and her new relationship with the Lord. She had become a Christian while he was gone and she shared her newly found faith with him. That Sunday Michelle's husband went to the altar and accepted the Lord. That night the couple shared with their huge church their entire marriage testimony. About a month later, they decided to renew their wedding vows.

~ Michelle in Florida, RESTORED

Update: The last time we heard from Michelle in Florida she was in a prolonged fast. She said that the Lord had impressed upon her heart to adopt her husband's baby girl. They had heard that the baby had been left for months with friends while the other woman went overseas. It seems that she had lost interest in her daughter soon after her lover had gone back to his wife.

"Husband Has a New and Broken Heart"

Phyllis came to a Restore Ministries fellowship meeting full of tears. Her marriage was over; her husband had filed for divorce. Three weeks later, her husband dropped the divorce and came home. He said he could not deny the complete change in his wife and now believed that things would "work out."

A few months later, her husband was given a job transfer, and their family was asked to move. However, her son was graduating from high school that year, so he didn't want to move with the family. So Phyllis asked her husband to give up his promotion so they could stay, but her husband said, "You choose; either come with me, or we're through."

Unfortunately, Phyllis chose to stay behind with her son and found herself legally divorced within three months. Despondent, she cried out to the Lord for help began applying the principles again. Two days later she found her *How God can and will Restore your Marriage* and *A Wise Woman* again and began poring over it with a new and broken heart.

This time, she said, the changes she made were real and permanent. Months later she wrote to tell us that she and her husband were remarried and have never been happier.

~ Phyllis in Florida, RESTORED again

Ministry Note: When the husband or wife has children from previous marriages, there are always many more opportunities for the enemy to use the children to divide and conquer the family. The real parent tends to protect or side with their own children instead of their spouse.

Chapter 6

Mary Ann

"... for we walk by faith,
not by sight!"
—2 Corinthians 5:7

"Reunited at the Altar"

We just heard a wonderful testimony about a couple who had been divorced for three years and hadn't seen each other for at least two. One night Mary Ann was invited to a revival service at a church in Pensacola, Florida (the church where the Thiele family attended for many years). When the altar call was given, she went to the altar and gave her live to the Lord. When they stood up she stood, she turned and saw her husband who had also gone to the altar and was saved that same night! When they saw one another they ran to embrace. Mary Ann and her husband were remarried shortly thereafter at the our church.

~ Mary Ann in Iowa, RESTORED

"Bankruptcy Brought Husband Home"

Chris, a woman with two teenagers, came to a Restore Ministries course when the fellowship met in Pensacola. Chris became entranced with Erin's books and the study every Monday. Each week she was open to the lessons in the workbook for women (not yet published) and embraced the teachings from *How God can and will Restore your Marriage*. However, one night the discussion focused on the fact that a man in adultery would be financially reduced to a loaf of bread and come to poverty. Chris refused to accept the principle and told Erin, "You obviously don't know my husband!" explaining that her husband was a financial genius, had an incredible job (one of the highest paid in their city), and that it was impossible for this to happen to him! She promptly stood up, and left the class and promised never to return.

About six months later, Chris humbly returned to the fellowship study with some news. Soon after she left the class, her husband lost his great job because of something the OW did. Then her husband used up all his savings, and even mortgaged the large home he had been by given his wife in the divorce in order to start a new business that had just gone bankrupt!

Chris began coming to the Monday classes, she said, with the mind and heart to accept every principle in *How God can and will Restore your Marriage* and the workbook for women. In complete poverty, this woman's husband eventually returned home to her and his children.

~ Chris in Florida, RESTORED

"Just Remarried"

Six months ago, our first publishers, Mt. Zion, received a phone call from a woman, Joanie, who said that she got *How God can and will Restore your Marriage* about a year ago and said she and her husband had been divorced for nine years. She said that she had not seen or heard from him during those nine years and Joanie went onto say she "didn't even know where he was living." But she said that when she read the book, she believed the promises that were written within the pages were for her.

Joanie said she had called to share her testimony with the publishers. Joanie said that she had just received an amazing phone call from her ex-husband. He said, "I called to tell you that I am interested in restoring our marriage. What do you think?" This woman thanked the publishers again and again for their part in helping to get *How God can and will Restore your Marriage* into the hands of those who need hope.

Praise the Lord! They were just remarried!!

~ Joanie in Delaware, RESTORED

Chapter 7

Tami

"A bed of sickness
... great tribulation,
unless they repent of her deeds"
—Revelations 2:21-22

"Changing Me!"

I have so much to thank the Lord for – I am not sure where to begin! This year has brought many changes in me, and I praise God for the work He is doing in me. It is a lifelong process -- I have finally realized that He does not expect me to change everything in the blink of an eye. A major blessing is the restoration of my youngest son's marriage. They were married one year, divorced for three years, and remarried last May. Now they are expecting their first child! This seemed impossible to the world, but God can do ANYTHING! He has given me peace and contentment and is healing our family - one piece at a time. Thank You, Father. Thank you, Erin, for your ministry. You are a continual blessing to all of us. I appreciate your honesty about your own struggles and trials. Satan does not want us to succeed, but God is for us—the victory is already His. In this special holiday time, let us be vigilant in our walk—we may bring Him the glory He deserves!

~ *Tami in Idaho*

"Marriage Restored after SEVEN Years of Separation!!"

A woman wrote that she ordered several "sets" of books from us to give out to those she met in marital crisis. She says she noticed something wonderful: that ALL those who "read and applied" QUICKLY got out of their marital trouble!!! Her most recent praise report was of a broken marriage that was just restored after SEVEN YEARS OF SEPARATION!! She wrote, "Praise the Lord, again, and thank you for this ministry!"

~ Polly in Wisconsin, RESTORED

Chapter 8

Jane

"I am well content with weaknesses,
with insults, with distresses,
with persecutions, with difficulties"
—2 Corinthians 12:10

"Restored in Five Months!!"

"And He has said to me, 'My grace is sufficient for you, for power is perfected in weakness.' Most gladly, therefore, I will rather boast about my weaknesses, so that the power of Christ may dwell in me. Therefore, I am well content with weaknesses, with insults, with distresses, with persecutions, with difficulties, for Christ's sake; for when I am weak, then I am strong" 2 Corinthians 12:9– 10.

The day my husband told me that he didn't love me anymore was the second worst day of my life! My husband had told me those same awful words before, five years prior to that day. At that time, through prayer and through God's amazing grace; we were restored after only five months!

However, five years later, to my dismay, my husband told me those awful words once again. I was distraught! I was feeling so low; I didn't even know what to say to God. I couldn't understand why God had done this to me again, why this would happen all over again!

As I humbled myself to the Lord, the Lord slowly began to show my why this HAD to happen. The last time I went through this, very soon, I slowly returned to my old ways—my old sinful ways. Even after I saw the miracle of my marriage restored, the miracle of my husband telling me that he loved me again, I slowly returned to my old habits and behaviors that DID NOT glorify the Lord.

The Lord made me see that the reasons were all my own. God had to change me once and for all! I felt so convicted, so ashamed, but at the same time I felt great comfort in knowing that God was not leaving me in this horrible pit; He was working in me and allowing me to see why this had to be!

I was searching on the internet for something, and all of a sudden I was on this amazing website, RMI. It was God leading me here! I read all of the materials over and over, and I purchased everything and kept my materials in my briefcase. Whenever I am waiting for a meeting to begin or have some time at work, I read through them, mark them and keep reading them again and again. It reminds me that everything is under God's control and also keeps my busy mind in check.

The site and PR are a great help to me that we have something in common with women traveling the same road. It is hard sometimes to stand alone believing for something that this world deems impossible!

Once I truly let God take my burden from me, things started to change! I did, unfortunately, listen to my friends who are Christians at first, but it was only making things much worse. They told me things that in my heart I knew were not right.

But once I started to surrender everything to the Lord, absolutely everything, I stared to receive the blessed gift of peace. I started to act differently towards my husband. I stopped trying to snoop for details, I stopped trying to show him how strong I was, I stopped trying to be perfect, and I stopped trying to please everyone! God's promises were for me and for my marriage!

What I learned was that God wanted and needed me to love Him with all of my heart, all of my mind, and all of my soul! I needed to love HIM the most. I finally had to realize that I had always loved my husband more than the Lord. I had to understand that the Lord was more than enough for me, no matter what happened—He was enough for me! Regardless if my husband came home or not (I believed he would), but I had to KNOW in my heart that the LORD alone was enough for me!

It was a truth that I had to learn and KNOW, that He would fill me up and that I would never feel lonely WITH HIM that I would never feel unloved *WITH* HIM. I had to know it! I remember one day driving in my car and I was feeling very sad that day because earlier that morning I had snooped in my husband's briefcase and had found that he looking into renting an apartment. I was devastated! I was crying and I remember so clearly, the song "More than Enough" was playing on the radio. I remember hearing the Lord say to me, "I AM MORE THAN ENOUGH for you." In that moment I felt so torn! I wanted the Lord, and yet I wanted my husband. Then I envisioned Jesus standing before me holding out His hand to me, and right beside him was my husband holding out his hand to me. I remember that I wanted to choose my husband! I remember feeling so ashamed that I wanted my husband more. I knew in my heart that I loved my husband more that I loved Jesus! How horrible.

Now I can honestly say, it has all changed, but He is Who had to change me. He had to show me that what I used to feel and believe was not right! The Lord wants and needs me to love Him best and the most! He is my all in all now, and I intend to keep it that way until the day I die! There were many terrible trials, so many sleepless nights. I remember distinctly, receiving phone calls telling me of details that ripped my heart out! I remember my husband telling me that I ruined his life, that I destroyed his dreams; that he never really loved me at all. But with each word spoken I felt the Lord whispering in my ear, "Jane, I love you, I love YOU." It was only God's grace and His deep love for me, that I was kept alive.

There were many times I wanted to die. I remember asking the Lord to take me home—I didn't want to live anymore. I had no children to love, I didn't have a husband who loved me; and I felt so alone! I felt so unworthy of love, but I knew deep down that God was in control. I realized that God was changing me, and that He was really all I could count on! I clung to the Lord, I clung to Him and let Him hold me—it was all that I could do.

As I began to really pray and fast, I began to build strength. I gained a confidence that I hadn't had before. It wasn't a boastful confidence—it was a quiet confidence that God was going to restore my marriage. I knew it would be in His timing and not mine! It was about 8 months into our trial that I began to really "see" the light. I needed to be humbled and reminded that I am not the "fixer" of anything. I needed to be pruned desperately and slowly I was dying to myself.

What I thought I needed and wanted during this time began to change. I was falling in the love with the Lord and I was realizing for the first time in my life that I truly LOVED the Lord! I knew in my heart that if that choice was offered again (Jesus or my husband), I would run to Jesus with open arms without hesitation! Even though I knew I still loved my husband in a lesser way, I just knew WHOM I would run to!!

The turning point was not just one event, it was several within a small period of time. It was in May, when my husband had come back to our bed. We still were nowhere near restored (I knew that), but this was huge; since he had moved into the guest bedroom in November! It was a major turning point, and I knew it!! He never said he loved me or anything like that, but I knew it was God! I was thankful and full of praise to Him.

I kept praying and fasting. Things were slowly improving, and then something would happen—and that's when I'd feel like things were going backwards! This went on all summer. But the more I prayed, the more confident I became to know that God was not going to leave me or stop working in us. And most importantly He loved me, the more I started replacing any doubt that came to my mind with praise and scripture, and I became a more peaceful person.

I started to like who I was! Even if I didn't have my husband's love, I knew My Lord loved me! That He would feed my soul and He replaced feelings of loneliness and despair, and it allowed me to feel safe and peaceful and loved.

In September, though I didn't want to go, I went to a Christian convention to hear a wonderful Christian woman speak. I had to go away for the weekend and I was nervous to go away because I wasn't sure what my husband would do when I went away! But when I prayed about it and I felt that He is who wanted me to go to this conference.

So, I went and He really spoke to me at this conference! I will never forget what happened! It was near the end of the conference, and this speaker said, "Who do you have confused with God? Who is it that has hurt you and made you feel that God is not trustworthy or truly worthy of your trust?" I remember crying my eyes out. I realized that in that moment, I wasn't completely trusting God for everything. I hadn't let go of it all because I felt as though God would end up hurting me, just as my husband had!

I remember sitting there at this conference with tears streaming down my face, submitting my life completely to Him and letting God heal my deepest wounds! I really felt in that moment, I changed! I started to really TRUST God. I had loved God and the Lord, and believed Him and His salvation—but I had to trust Him, really trust Him. After all, He had never lied to me or hurt me. So I guess I was just waiting for Him to break promises to me or leave me. When I started to let all of that go, I realized that He NEVER would! He wasn't my husband or any man for that matter, He was God, the Great I AM!! I wasn't dealing with just anyone, IT WAS GOD HIMSELF who gave me His Son, a faithful Husband. I was in awe and felt so much love inside me, I was overwhelmed.

On the way home from that conference, my husband called me on the phone and seemed so happy to talk to me! We had plans to go to a concert that night. After the concert, on the way home in the car, my husband said to me, "I am so glad that you are strong. Thank you for staying strong for us." Then he proceeded to tell me that he wanted to try and have a baby with me!! (He has always said he didn't want to have children). He said that he wanted to make our family concrete! I remember sitting there in shock, but also filled with love and an overwhelming gratitude to the Lord.

Even though he hadn't told me that he loved me, I knew that we were close. I knew restoration wasn't complete yet, but I knew it was a GIANT step. I kept praising God and believing that it would come, but if not, I still had and wanted Him more. The next day my husband left for a 28 day business trip. As I dropped him off at the airport, he held me in his arms and said, "I love you." I felt the tears well up and I knew that God was restoring us. I remember whispering "I love you" back to him.

It had been almost one year to the date when this restoration happened. It was a miracle! During his absence things got a bit rocky, and I felt satan really trying to destroy us. I prayed and prayed! God is good and reassured me many times! My husband came home and was a little aloof for awhile, but I had the Lord who I cared about most, while God continued to change me, change us and through His mighty glory, my husband up and tells me that he loves me.

Now that we are fully restored, he has begun to talk to me the way the way I always wanted him too. He is affectionate with me and wears his wedding ring all the time. I can only say that it will be a constant battle with satan for my marriage, I know that. I know that I will trust God for my marriage and my husband until the day I die, but I know that God is faithful. He hears our prayers and loves our spouses so much more than we ever could!

I also know that God HAD to change me. He had to get my attention and HE had to do it the way He did. God is sovereign and righteous. Until I loved His Son, my real Husband the most, He couldn't leave me in that state. I am thankful for His goodness and for His mighty works. God IS a God of miracles!! He saved our marriage! My husband wanted a divorce, but now he wants us to try and have a baby with me! He holds me and tells me he loves me. I know that God is GOOD and I believe that God has a plan for all of us.

My husband is changing and I know that I am still changing too. God needs me to be who He wants me to be as His Son's bride. I understand it now, and I fully give God all the glory and all the credit. It is God all the way, and I know that I must constantly keep my love for my husband in check. I know that I can ever let anything or anyone come between me and the Lord again.

I need the Lord more than anything else in my life! I LOVE HIM more than I ever thought I could. I am so thankful that I know this now; I sing love songs to the Lord, for He is SO good as a Husband! Amen!!

~ Jane in Michigan, Fellowship Member, RESTORED!

Ministry Note: Jane's daughter turned 5 years old, and her 2nd restoration baby, we heard, was a boy! :)

Chapter 9

Rachel

"The reward of humility and
the fear of the Lord
are riches, honor and life"
—Proverbs 22:4

"Firefighters Getting Married!"

Then, Glory to God, two months later a young woman came up and asked my husband what his name was. When he told her, she began to share that she was the mother of the man's baby whom my husband spoke to. She said that he had, for weeks, been looking for him to tell him how his life had changed. This woman said several times "He is just not the same man!!!" She said that he is a truck driver and now everywhere he goes he meets Christian men. She also said that he had been going regularly to church and was attending a Sunday school our church offers for new Christians to be discipled!

Then she showed us her hand with her engagement ring. "We're getting married!!" she said!!

Praise the Lord for His faithfulness!!!

They were married at our church in a small informal ceremony.

~ Rachel RESTORED in Missouri

Pastor Blessed with Restored Marriage!!

A pastor contacted RMI for help. His wife had recently left him. She simply said that she didn't love him anymore. Of course, he was very distraught so he ordered *How God Will Restore Your Marriage* for men and the men's manual *A Wise Man*. He said he studied and pored over the material again and again. He contacted Encouraging Men several times for support and guidance, but we continued to encouraged him to get what He needed from the Lord. Then then we stopped hearing from him, and after several months we got the news—his marriage had been restored!! Hallelujah!!!

He said that his wife had returned home several months earlier (probably when he stopped contacting our ministry), but he was so caught up in his new life with his wife that he had failed to contact us!

What was such a surprise was that his wife was so pleased with the ministry that she was who we saw order cases of books and workbooks for women regularly! Pastor Joseph said he and his wife use our materials to help other couples in crisis and to use in their Sunday school classes. When his wife orders, she often sends a note. The most recent simply said, "Praise God for your ministry!" So that's when we realized it was Pastor Joseph's wife and each time she orders we're doubly blessed!

~ Pastor Joseph RESTORED in Florida

Chapter 10

Patrice

"A broken and a contrite heart,
O God, You will not despise."
— Psalm 51:17

"Broken in Alabama"

At a homeschool one of the moms noticed that one of the other mothers who was a regular at their homeschool meetings had lost a lot of weight. However, later when she complimented her, Patrice broke down in tears, saying it was because she "couldn't eat." Her husband had left her and her six children six weeks earlier! Thankfully the homeschool mom had heard about *How God Can and Will Restore Your Marriage* from another home school mom who was now in a restored marriage. So she told her to ask that friend for it.

When she saw the small book, she doubted that it could help her. However, when she read through it, she found that it answered all the questions she had, and with Biblical answers. In the past she had often tried to "fix" their marriage troubles with her husband based on other marriage books she read or advice from her friends. And she said, "Everything that she'd tried made things worse." Patrice was so desperate for the truth, and when she read the verses, she knew she had finally found it.

Patrice said it didn't take long to read through the book several times; each time she said that she became aware of something new. The turning point is when she said she stopped "trying" to get her husband to come back, but concentrated on the verses of Scripture that she highlighted in her Bible.

In less than three weeks, when her husband finally came around to see the children, he was amazed at the change in his wife. She had lost over 50 pounds since he had left over two months earlier! But the most amazing change, he later said, was her countenance and personality. The once angry contentious woman was now sweet, gentle and kind to him even though he had left her without even a good-bye!

After a full day of observing her, to make sure it was real, he decided to stay the night. Her husband never left again!!

One Sunday morning the homeschool mom, who had told her about the book, saw the entire family of eight eating breakfast at a local restaurant. They were attending a new church and she said the entire family looked so different—once sort of a sad looking family—they were happy and laughing together!

~ Patrice in Alabama, RESTORED

"Another Marriage Restored in Florida!"

We just spoke to a couple in Florida. They have a restored marriage due to the wife reading and applying the *Restore Your Marriage* book!!! Our publisher called and asked us to call them. They had contacted our publishers to ask permission to translate the book into Spanish since she wanted a Spanish version for all the ladies she knows who can't read English. (The Lord did not use this couple for the Spanish translation, but instead a professional translating ministry did it for us!.)

They promised to email us their complete testimony but unfortunately, we never got it.

~ Peggy and Juan RESTORED in Florida

"Brought to Tears Restored 'Suddenly'!!"

After two years, "suddenly" a young married woman wanted to stop the divorce proceedings she initiated against her husband and work things out!!! She said that she didn't know how or why but her feelings for her husband had returned. Her mother in-law contacted us who has been believing God for the restoration of of her son's marriage said, "I am just amazed and awed by the power of the Lord Jesus Christ!"

Aren't we all?!! Praise the Lord for His faithfulness to His Word and His Promises!! Don't let ANYONE tell you that God cannot or will not turn the heart of your spouse or family members. He does it ALL THE TIME!!! Who cares about the will of man, when God in His mercy created all of us with a heart that HE TURNS whatever way He wishes?!?!

Barb wrote, "We had such a precious weekend, two full days with my husband. We literally spent most of the weekend side by side. He had me over for dinner Saturday night and then again Sunday night. Later, both nights I ended up staying with him. However...THE ULTIMATE thing happened Saturday before we went to sleep. He said, 'We should pray.' He took my hand and he prayed and thanked God for His working in our lives. This brings me to tears."

~ Barb in North Carolina, RESTORED

Chapter 11

Alexy

"A broken and a contrite heart,
O God, You will not despise."
—Psalm 51:17

"My World had Come to an End"

Alexy how did your restoration actually begin?

First of all I thank this ministry for allowing God to minister to the brokenhearted and to restore marriages through RMI. The day my EH confessed and told me there was someone else and he no longer loved me, that automatically brought me to my knees and reminded me of how i was the cause... i was unfaithful to God. i just kept crying for 3 days without food asking God to forgive me.

The pain that i felt i knew God felt that pain when i chose my EH (back then my boyfriend) over Him and i backslid. And because of that guilt, I kept crying. I totally lost my appetite and wanted to commit suicide: the thought of the disappointment in the faces of my children knowing i had committed suicide kept me from doing it. I wanted them to know that i loved them and doing that would seem to them as rejection, so i prayed to God to take my life and I lay on my bed to sleep hoping not to wake up.

But God be praised, i woke up the next day with that pain in my heart, in fact, as i was sleeping i could feel it. I had never felt such pain, and over the next days i kept wondering how i could separate myself from that pain. At that moment that was the most painful realization (me breaking the heart of God in that manner and my EH doing the same to me). I knew you reap what you sow and that verse kept ringing in my head and then cursed is the man who puts their trust in another man verse. I had trusted my EH so much that i was in too much pain and shock that i wanted to die, in fact, i preferred to die BECAUSE I THOUGHT MY WORLD HAD COME TO AN END.

Prior to meeting my EH I was so in love with the LORD as a young girl and on meeting my EH i turned my back to the truth that i knew and did fornicate, which led to pregnancy and eventually cohabiting with my EH; six years later we officially married. AND my excuse for everything was 1 Cor 7:16 knowing that my faith would save my spouse even when i was warned that darkness cannot meet with light by most of my spiritual brethren. I honestly believed this verse and quoted it for myself. So now i look back and i know that i was only gratifying my flesh. Upon examining myself more, i realized that i did not trust God. i got me a born again husband, so i did it my way. Several times during my journey i kept repenting of not trusting God and that is what kept me on my restoration journey because my flesh wanted the easiest way out of this situation and i thought walking away would do it.

How did God change your situation as you sought Him wholeheartedly Alexy?

God started changing my situation when i learned to let go and stop pursuing and calling my EH and especially having a gentle and quiet spirit. In fact i started to give up anything that was irritating my EH. I kept myself busy even whenever my EH was around, this helped me not to talk unnecessary things or words that i would regret later.

GENTLE AND QUIET SPIRIT is golden that was the winner. i would welcome my EH even when he'd come home in the wee hours of the morning without complaining, warm his meal and prep his bath, then excuse myself without a word and if he did not want anything, then i would still excuse myself because he never wanted to be with me in the same room. When he noticed i was giving him his space that's when he wanted to be around me. He started saying i was doing that to get back at him, yet he never realized how much pain it took me to do that.

What principles, from God's Word (or through our resources), did the Lord teach you during this trial Alexy?

The golden rule: gentle and a quiet spirit. not slandering my husband are what i learned through this ministry. Looking at my sin, not on others, also helped me look to God. Above all Love is what i have learned as God kept speaking to me to love my EH as God loves me. My lovely sisters, this journey was the most painful, hard but also the most rewarding AS I GOT TO KNOW GOD FROM ANOTHER DIMENSION!

Alexy what were the most difficult times that God helped you through?

While I was expecting my fourth child, it was hard to go through with pregnancy in those circumstances, but again God saw me through and even the time i was giving birth i gave birth like a Hebrew woman PTL. I actually prayed that my EH would not be there and he was not. I didn't want him because he would call and talk to OW in my presence or excuse himself to talk on phone to OW, which was painful to me.

The other difficult times was when my EH would go to work early Monday morning and come back on Saturday night, with the rest of the days he would be spending with OW. It was painful but i learned to be quiet and gentle in that and actually kind to my EH. Also the many times he would talk on phone to OW in my presence.

Then my children would all fall sick at once, that was really a trying time and people at my place of work would not understand at all and i would have no one to help me apart from my maid who was like an angel at that time. BUT God saw me through it all. i was so afraid of my home while still under construction; that place was dark and i feared it so genuinely that was afraid to move to the house. but when all my troubles poured on me the fear just vanished i don't know how but i started getting a welcome feeling from that place as our home and i felt that was the only place i could run to... that is how i ended up moving to our present home without fear, God used my situation to get me to move to my home.

What was the "turning point" of your restoration Alexy?

When my EH got involved in a motor accident that totaled his car, he started coming home everyday though we were not yet in good talking terms. he still came home every day and even very late every night. It was painful and i thought it would never end BUT eventually he started coming home the earliest he has ever been doing and spending a lot of time at home. His heart started turning more to home and towards the children. so many times i wanted to give up because things were not happening the way i wanted and at the pace that i wanted.

i made many mistakes BUT God overlooked all my flaws. I look back and i regret that i did not trust God so much and i regret not Loving my EH in his sin the way God would have wanted me to. I realized that i also had not forgiven him on several accounts.

Tell us HOW it happened? Did your husband just walk in the front door?

Yes, he did! I actually got used to my EH coming home on Saturday night, but the night of my restoration, this time he came on Friday; i was thrilled and expressed it to him, he just smiled and my restoration was complete.

Did you suspect or could you tell you were close to being restored?

No, I did not suspect that it was about to happen, but i knew it would happen eventually. i was expecting things to get harder as a few months prior, i woke up singing "though i walk through the valley of the shadow of death i will fear no evil for thou art with me" in my dream so i was expecting worse things but PTL He brought me through.

Alexy would you recommend any of our resource in particular that helped you?

How God can and will Restore your Marriage was really the best with all the principles.

By the Word of Their Testimony AND Be Encouraged eVideos.

Do you have favorite Bible verses that you would like to pass on to women reading your Testimonies? Promises that He gave you?

Joel 2:25

“I will repay you for the years the locusts have eaten—

the great locust and the young locust,

the other locusts and the locust swarm —

my great army that I sent among you.”

Esther 6:13

“His advisers and his wife Zeresh said to him, ‘Since Mordecai, before whom your downfall has started, is of Jewish origin, you cannot stand against him—you will surely come to ruin!’”

Would you be interested in helping encourage other women?

Yes i feel i need to encourage other women!

Dear Friend,

Surrender to God this trial, is not a mistake, He planned it to happen this way so that you would learn to lean and trust in Him and if your EH is gone, that you stop looking to your EH. I loved the book of Esther it encouraged me to know how when we sincerely repent wholeheartedly, God will turn our tables around. Read Esther often. To me this book is prophetic. Also pray for a gentle and quiet spirit because it’s golden— not only for your restoration but for your good AND APPLY THESE from all the books, these PRINCIPLES— THEY ARE WISDOM!

Here is one of Alexy’s PR she submitted exactly a year before.

I am just so blessed that i found this ministry. First and foremost i don't know where i would be if i had not stumbled on this ministry. It is my first time to write a praise report but there is so much to praise God for. I found RMI WHEN I WAS TORN and broken a few month (three) after my EH made a hurtful confession after he could not hide anything from me any more and along with that told me how he felt about me and how we could never be happy together.

Now since finding you, i feel more complete and whole for my hope was on sinking sand and now I'm on the solid Rock!

One night out of pain i got a knife and gave him and i told him to kill me instead of treating me the way that he had been, this was after i had contemplated suicide then i asked God to kill so that way no one would know what and why i was dead. PTL I am alive today more vibrant than ever and longing for God.

I was four months pregnant when this journey begun in that pregnancy I lost fifteen kilograms (33 lbs.) and by the time i was back to work from maternity leave, everyone was asking me how i managed to loose all that weight! I was speechless because i did not know i had lost all that weight though i knew i had shed some weight, which i had struggled to lose for many years.

I have three children and this was my fourth pregnancy but the childbirth in the absence of my husband was an amazingly very short labor. The nurses were the best i got a very comfortable room in the hospital —i felt the Love of God. My baby, without any exaggeration, is the most jolly baby i ever had yet throughout my pregnancy. Even though i cried (i had never cried so much in my life and was afraid my baby would be a moody boy) but PTL of all the children i have, this son has taught me how to laugh and praise God!! I have never seen another baby that laughs, dances and claps hands like my baby. This little boy looks for an opportunity in everything to laugh and be joyful—surely he is a blessing and he teaches me to rejoice.

God had clearly spoken to me in a dream about my situation to rejoice and not to look at my circumstances, but instead *worshiped* my pain and rejection. I was so blind that i thought it was unrealistic for me to rejoice at that moment.

Then i met RMI—YOU GAVE ME GUIDELINES ON HOW TO DO SO MANY THINGS GOD HAD SPOKEN TO ME ABOUT. Without RMI i think i would have failed and gotten stuck in that pain—BUT thank You Erin for letting God use you this way!! You have really encouraged me and brought me out of my pain, guiding me as in the hand of God.

Discovering certain things about my responsibility in this situation has been very painful, but PTL i know He has changed me. I have been plagued by falling many times because i didn't want to accept certain correction and besides that i don't know how to do things any other way.

But now i am deeply yearning for God to pour out a spirit of obedience up on me. All i want now is to do His will. In this journey, my dear sisters, in all the praise Reports i have read He is longing to do this to all who accept and drink from Him—for Jesus is the same yesterday, today, and forever!! Praise His name forever!!

"Beauty for Ashes"

I am just so blessed that I found this ministry. First and foremost, I don't know where I would be if I had not "stumbled" on this ministry. It is my first time to write a praise report but there is so much to praise God for. I found RMI WHEN I WAS TORN and broken a few months (three) after my EH made a hurtful confession after he could not hide anything from me any more, and along with that told me how he felt about me and how we could never be happy together. Now I feel more complete and whole for my hope was on sinking sand but now it is on the Solid ROCK. One night, out of pain I got a knife and gave it to him and I told him to kill me instead of treating me that way. That was after I had contemplated suicide, then I asked God to kill me so that way no one would know for what and why I was dead. PTL!!! I am ALIVE today more vibrant than ever and longing for God.

I was four months pregnant when this journey begun. In that pregnancy I lost fifteen kilograms and by the time I was back to work from maternity leave, everyone was asking me how I managed to lose all that weight. I was speechless, I did not know I had lost all that weight though I knew I had shed some weight that I had struggled to lose for many years. I have three children and this was my fourth pregnancy but the child birth, in the absence of my husband, was amazingly a very short labor! The nurses were the best and I got a very comfortable room in the hospital. I felt the Love of God. My baby, without any exaggeration, is the most jolly baby I ever had yet. Throughout my pregnancy I cried. I had never cried so much in my life and was afraid my baby would be a moody boy, but PTL of all the children I have, he has taught me how to laugh and praise God. I have never seen another baby that laughs, dances and claps hands like my baby. He looks for an opportunity in everything to laugh and be joyful. Surely he is a blessing and he teaches me to rejoice.

God had clearly spoken to me in a dream about my situation and told me to rejoice and not to look at my circumstances, but I worshiped my pain and rejection. I was so blind that I thought it was unrealistic for me to rejoice at that moment. Then I met RMI!! YOU GAVE ME GUIDELINES ON HOW TO DO SO MANY THINGS GOD HAD SPOKEN TO ME ABOUT. Without RMI I think I would have failed and got stuck in that pain. BUT thank You Erin for letting God use you this way. You have really encouraged me and brought me out, guiding me as in the hand of God.

Discovering certain things about my responsibility in this situation has been very painful, but PTL I know He has changed me. I have been plagued by failing many times because I didn't want to accept certain correction and besides that, I don't know how to do things any other way. But now I am deeply yearning for God to pour out a spirit of obedience up on me. All I want now is to do His will. In this journey my dear sisters, in all the praise Reports I have read, He is longing to do this to all who accept to drink from Him for Jesus is the same yesterday, today and forever!! Praise His name forever!!

~ *Alexy in Uganda*

Chapter 12

Rose

"A broken and a contrite heart,
O God, You will not despise."
—Psalm 51:17

"Reduced to a Slice of Bread"

My parents were divorced after my father had committed adultery with a lady at work and decided to leave his family. Several years later, I bought *How God can and will Restore your Marriage* and the workbook for women *Wise Woman* for my marriage because I knew it was shaky. As I read the books, I thought how wonderful it would be if my parents "got back together." After read both books a couple of times (probably more) and then felt impressed to pray, "Lord, whatever it takes, bring my father back home to my mother!" What it took was my father losing everything! The first to go was his health when began failing him, then he lost all his money. That's when his girlfriend left him, and finally the trailer he lived in burned down — my father actually left the burning trailer wearing only his pajamas and a robe! He lost everything he owned in the trailer!

When my father called his ex-wife, my mom, from the police station, I was there with her. When my mom got off the phone she said, "he finally ask me for forgiveness"!

~ Rose in Kentucky, RESTORED

Ministry Note: Erin was blessed to see a picture of this happy couple together at their recent wedding standing between their five grown and married daughters, which we were asked not to make public.

"My Mom Returns Home after her Fifth Husband!"

I'm submitting this testimony for my mom. She'd told all of us that her marriage to my dad had never been what she had hoped. Soon after her second child, my sister, she began looking around at other men. It led to her thinking about, but never committing adultery. But as soon as the last of us was in college, and her "children were grown" my mom said her inhibitions diminished. One night she did what she had been thinking of for years—she committed adultery. Soon my mom and my separated, and not too long afterwards, divorced.

My mom moved in with the other man she'd met, but the relationship soon ended. So my mom said, she looked around again, began sleeping with another man, soon moved in with him, but again, it was over very soon. Then she met a fourth man... this time it eventually led to the altar. They married. My mom had hoped that the marriage would help us, her children, to accept this new man, since each man she tried to make us meet, we had refused to acknowledge the other three men. My siblings and I both of us are married and have children, so we lovingly refused to allow my to bring any men into either of our homes. From the beginning, we would meet with my mom alone and, in spite of everything she'd done, loved her unconditionally. But these men, married to my mother or not, were not our father, nor our children's grandfather. No men my mother was involved with had anything to do with us, so we agreed that by "accepting" them as part of our family would be dishonoring my father.

This put strain on my mom's new marriage and very soon, it ended in divorce. But my mom wouldn't stop, soon she became involved with and married two more men. But, finally it happened as we warned her it would. My mom's fifth husband began beating my mom violently, and she ended up in the emergency room. When my mom called, we all came to the hospital and lovingly asked my mother, "Mom, when are you going to repent and ask Dad to forgive you? How much more will it take?"

My mom asked us to call my dad. My dad came into the room and almost didn't recognize my mom, but he did hear the words he had only dreamed about (my dad had remained single hoping for my mom to someday return home to him.)

I'm thrilled to say that my parents remarried and now we are able to be together for holidays and all our birthdays, all three generations, as a complete and healed family. THANK YOU GOD!!!

~ Jessica whose parents also live in Florida, RESTORED

Chapter 13

Bunny

"A broken and a contrite heart,
O God, You will not despise."
— Psalm 51:17

"My EH's Girlfriend Had a Dream"

I read a similar testimony from RMI when I first came that I was fascinated by, but never imagined I'd ever submit one myself so much the same. One night I woke up a desperate feeling to pray for the OW my husband was involved with. I'd had been desperately seeking help for my own marriage and had purchased and had started reading and rereading *How God Will Restore Your Marriage* and the workbook for women (this was before the courses were available). So it was crazy because that day was the third day of my fasting, so as the book says and on the fast, I'd been praying the prayers in the back of the RYM book over and over. The night I got that urge to pray, I was surprised I was able to stay up all night until the sun came up. Yes I was exhausted, but I soon fell asleep for a couple of hours until my alarm went off to go to work.

That very day I received an angry phone call from my husband at work, the OW who had left him! So very angry, yelling, he shouted why I had gotten in touch with his girlfriend. Thankfully I could honestly say, "I never contacted her, not ever" and asked why he was asking me. He told my that his girlfriend had come into his office that morning, shouted and said they "were through" and then it was the OW that began rambling something about him "lying" about my wife. My EH said he'd told she didn't want him anymore, which my husband knew was far from the truth. Unfortunately being part of a standers ministry in the beginning I was very vocal about our marriage covenant and about how God was going to bring him home, but that made him move out and in with his girlfriend and not speak to me again. So I was shocked when he called me at work.

My EH went on to say his girlfriend didn't stop there by telling him off and breaking up. The OW marched in and confessed their relationship to their boss (it is against office policy since he's her boss) and she demanded to be transferred.

Again I assured my EH that I had not said a thing, nor did my friends or family because I cut all of them off when I began my RJ knowing they would tell me things that went against the bible. So my EH hung up, not angry with me, but still very shaken and not knowing how this would affect his job.

Two days later he called again after hearing the whole story from a fellow coworker. It seems that on the very night I felt the urge to pray, my EH's girlfriend had a terrifying dream. In her dream she said she, "I saw his wife crying because she wanted her husband back." When she woke up, she was so shaken she didn't think she could make it to work that day but went anyway. And as soon as she clocked in, she went straight to the coffee room she asked another woman if she knew what their boss's wife looked like. When the woman began to describe her, this girl began to shake again. The description of his wife was exactly the wife in her dream who was crying. The girlfriend told her boss that she was totally "spooked" by the whole ordeal and wanted to get as far away as she could.

When my EH heard the full story it sent my husband back to God with a new and permanent "fear of the Lord" he said. It totally changed him and now he is fully committed to me and our children.

~ Bunny in Mississippi, RESTORED

"He Saw Her Wonderful Change"

A month ago, I emailed RMI for help and bought a *How God Will Restore Your Marriage* and was very encouraged about my marriage. So I began sharing the book with several others I knew were either separated or divorced, and I began a local meeting for everyone in our company who needed help. At first we had men too, but then heard how dangerous that could be so we started meeting on different days.

Then one night at my church, I met a woman who told her that her husband had just filed for divorce. Later I saw her again and she said she'd been reading *How God Will Restore Your Marriage*, and as I suggested, she also purchased the workbook for women from Amazon. So I was shocked when she went on to say that her husband commented on the "wonderful change" he saw in her and.... he decided to drop the divorce proceedings and move back home. What began with just me, then our company, has now spread to helping women in my church! I'm not sure how they will react since I know my pastor is on a second or third marriage and thinks trying to restore a marriage is wrong. So I hadn't said much, only very carefully to woman I felt I needed to share the truth with. Who knew our GOD would use me just being willing to open up and share the truth with women I knew might want to hear the truth!!

~ *Madeline in Kansas, RESTORED*

Chapter 14

James and Nita

"A broken and a contrite heart,
O God, You will not despise."
— Psalm 51:17

"My Wife's Boyfriend's Gone"

My wife and I are now back TOGETHER!! After I found himself divorced and living alone in my own apartment without my wife and children, I knew I had to do something RADICAL to change the way I was! So while on the internet I saw the RMI men's restoration book and I absorbed every concept and principle, basically I "ran" with them just like I do when I run each morning. I read and taped portions, then played them, hearing myself tell myself the truth over and over. Then I'd read more.

When my wife had first left me to find her own apartment, was so angry, she wouldn't speak or even look at me. So the first step was to somehow let her know that I had "let go" as your ministry advised. It was tricky because as I said, she wanted nothing to do with me, so I prayed (like the book or somewhere on your site says to do) and God orchestrated a random meeting when I ran into her. I was brief but was clear she was free to go, I was moving on and I was happy about her new boyfriend. Wow, almost immediately she stopped trying to get away from me. She stayed standing there and we talked for several minutes.

A few weeks later I found out that my wife had trouble finding a baby-sitter when she went out on a date with her new boyfriend, so I offered to baby-sit. This wasn't my idea, but GOD's. He told me if I loved her (and of course I loved my children) so why not offer. This was the opportunity from God that I asked for, but nothing like I wanted it to happen! Each night that I had an "opportunity" to baby-sit soon after I got the children into bed, I kept busy cleaning up the house. I'd run the vacuum first (since the children weren't asleep yet) then I'd start the washer or fold laundry that was on the couch. Next I'd do the dishes that had been left piled high in the sink. If I told anyone I know what they'd say about me so I didn't tell anyone. The truth was, I was determined to go the second, third, or even the fourth mile just like the bible says to do.

Other than reading my bible and my RYM book, I had nothing in my life, so I was "always be available" whenever my wife called. The truth is that at first it hurt so much to see my wife together with someone else (there were plenty of men) but hey, my children have been through a lot and I cherished every moment that I could spend with them. So that was my main focus when I would want to quit this whole thing because none of this seemed to phase my wife at all. She sort of acted as if this was expected of me, so it took a lot of humility on my part, asking myself "what would Jesus do?"

Well, God never fails, His word is true and His promises will be fulfilled if you believe and act them out radically! God blessed me for my heart of humility and service toward my wife. Not long after I fought wanting to quit, my wife's newest boyfriend started to become irritated with me always being in her apartment when they got home from their date. Her boyfriend started to becoming rude and was so arrogant, trying to pick a fight me. But I told my wife I'd never again respond to anything in anger (it was the reason she left me) so no matter what I had to respond with kindness and accept each insult he threw at me.

After a few more of these attacks, my wife stood up for me!! Three weeks later after another incident when he tried to pick a fight, my wife ordered her boyfriend out of the house and said as she slammed the screen door, "...and don't come back!"

I didn't know what to say. That's when my wife said that she could no longer deny the radical change in me. She knew that the change in me was real. She said that when I first came she thought I was just trying to get her back so she actually tried to make me break.

It was just a few months later we remarried again! Glory to God!! I know this testimony should have been sent years ago. But it's been many years and when I referred a friend I was sad to see that Coke had passed so I never got a chance to thank him for the letters he wrote for all of us and the example he set.

~ James and Nita in Indiana, RESTORED for years

Chapter 15

Paige

"A broken and a contrite heart,
O God, You will not despise."
— Psalm 51:17

"Miscarriages Tore Us Apart!"

My testimony begins shortly after my husband and I had only been married a short time. We were both excited that I had become pregnant right away but unfortunately it resulted in a horribly tragic miscarriage. Soon after by only a few months I found out I was expecting again but again I carried this baby only two short months before I miscarried again.

My husband and I were living overseas because my husband was in the military. It helped both of us to find close friends, a another military couple that lived on base, that my husband and I became very close to.

Soon as before only a few months later I was again expecting for the third time. This time both of us were very hopeful since I made it to the end of my second trimester. Then one night I fell asleep on the couch while our friends were visiting late. When I woke, I was paralyzed with shock....there across the room was my husband and the other woman kissing!! Her husband had apparently gone home and left his wife and my husband alone. Needless to say panic struck hard and I was shocked I hadn't even screamed or yelled out. Not knowing what to do I decided to move around to alert them that I was waking up, I saw them both jumped apart and then they pretending that nothing had happened.

The next morning after my husband left I contacted my in-laws because they were Christians and they began to pray with me. Suddenly in less than a week my husband was transferred back to our hometown for more training at a local military base. God had intervened just as my FIL had prayed would happen! So being away from this couple I thought my whole nightmare was over until I noticed an email from the other woman addressed to my husband. I almost fell over when I read the love letter that included a plan for them to "run away together after the baby is born"! My head began spinning... so again I called my in-laws for help and was relieved they had personally called the head of Restore Ministries.

I didn't know that they'd been close friends years before and it's why they knew what to do. Within two days, they had given me the *How God Will Restore Your Marriage* and also women's workbook that they told me I must read. They told me they'd both read and reread the books for years and it was my only hope. God could intervene but that He wanted me to know His truth. I'd never believed in God much, but right now I knew I needed something.

So I was surprised that my FIL went against the principles in the book and he insisted on confronting his son about his behavior against what my MIL said. My MIL didn't try to stop him, but right after this ugly truth was out, it only encouraged my husband to outwardly pursue the woman he then said he felt he was "in love" with!! When they contacted Restore Ministries again, Erin simply told them, it was clear that they would need a miracle and only God could and would fix my marriage.

My miracle came after much prayer, much crying and after our first baby was born. My husband wasn't there but soon after our daughter was born, my husband agreed to go to church with his parents (we were separated). That night he went again and I heard that he ran to the altar and he repented his sin of adultery to God and stood up with a new heart toward me.

~ Paige in Florida, RESTORED

Update: Paige and her husband have three little children now. They had a temporary setback about a year after their miracle when the other woman resurfaced in their lives. Paige confessed that she had "backslidden" and stopped following the principles in the RYM and workbook. But as soon as the OW showed up again, it sent her back to her reading and rereading everything with a renewed spirit! Paige said she would be staying in the book for her entire live, which has caused her to walk the principles out daily to protect her marriage from adultery she said. Thank you Lord!!

Chapter 16

Renea

"A broken and a contrite heart,
O God, You will not despise."
— Psalm 51:17

"My Husband Wanted to Date Other People"

I contacted RMI after I'd been married only a few short months. I was deeply distressed because my husband began staying out all night with "the boys." When I tried to confront him about it, I found him to be unresponsive and even hostile. Soon he announced that we should begin dating other people. I knew then that there was another woman involved. Right after we married we stopped going to church. So when I tried to pray, I felt guilty and unworthy; however, I didn't know what else to do or where to turn. Two days later I found myself at a conference on home schooling a Divine Appointment as HopeAtLast.com says!

Since I had no children I couldn't understand WHY I had even gone there! Soon after the meeting started I decided to leave, but then, when the speaker began to share her testimony of her restored marriage I just knew that the Lord had heard my prayers for help!!! When the speaker finished, I ran to the product table and bought both *How God can and will Restore your Marriage* and the women's workbook *A Wise Woman*.

That night I realized that my marriage had been built on sinking sand and it had fallen.

It took diligence and faith to endure the next several months when my husband filed for divorce. However, my husband could not deny the changes he saw in me! Nevertheless, he did everything he could to push me away. He dated new women, flaunting them in front of my face and calling after his late dates to tell me all the details I DID NOT WANT TO HEAR. His goal, my EH said later, was to make me hate him. But by then I had my HH love and nothing my EH could do would affect me. I remained quiet and focused on my new Love.

Things got worse, but I refused to contest or fight my husband about the divorce. Frustrated, he dropped the divorce. He said he "felt guilty because I wouldn't fight back." A few months later the Lord used a tragedy in my EH own personal life as his "wake-up call" he said crying. My EH best friend took his life. After the shock, my EH called me and repented of his regrets because of his unfaithfulness to me and to their marriage.

Today, eight years later, we are still "very happily married" and have TWO precious little girls who Renea homeschools. Restoration Babies RMI calls them. We both agree how wonderful it is to know that we are now together forever and that neither of us ever thinks or speaks of leaving as we used to.

~ Renea in Montana, RESTORED

UPDATE: Renea and her husband were one of the first RMI restored marriages. Their girls are grown now and recently they renewed their wedding vows in the church where they'd first gotten married.

Chapter 17

Vicky

"A broken and a contrite heart,
O God, You will not despise."
— Psalm 51:17

"My Victory"

First, Vicky from Kenya just submitted her Restored Marriage testimony. When I wrote to her about the new member in Kenya, she wrote me back with this:

Hello Erin,

It is so good to hear from you. I have been doing well in the Lord and have really seen His glorious and mighty hand in my life. He has really been good to me. In all my trials He has been my strong hold. I have continued to patiently to wait for Him. I have gone through lots of trials like, I was told I was to go back to work a few days after your visit but it never happened. I receive a call from my boss that I was to be laid-off. It has been stressing but I continue to praise God. Though at times I ask myself so many questions (I have been jobless for many months) I am still hoping for a miracle.

It's not easy considering my husband is jobless too, but I am not complaining because God gave me what I have really been praying for, my HUSBAND! YES, he came back home six months ago, and said that he was sorry and that he want us to bring up our children together. I have not posted my restoration yet because he said the same thing once before but left after a month. I didn't want to be anxious, but I promise to be submitting my testimony very soon.

I have been observing him and have seen a lot of change in him. About Milka I will call her and meet now that I have a lot of time.

Otherwise, may God give you a rainbow for every storm, a smile for every tear, a blessing for each trial, a sweet praise for a sign, and an answer for every prayer. God bless you and your ministry. Miss you.

~ *Vicky in Kenya*

My response was:

Hello Vicky!!!

I am so glad you wrote and told me what has been happening in your life!!! After I read that your husband was home, and you are both out of work, I felt led to wire you some money as a gift, but when I checked what I had to give you, it was not as much as I wanted to send.

What I feel that the Lord would have me to do is to ask that you submit your restored marriage testimony and then I can post it with a link for the ladies to also have the opportunity to give to you and your husband as a blessing from the Lord. They will be able to use their credit cards, and then I can wire the money order via Western Union to you. I have done it before when I sent a widow some money in Tanzania, Africa. If you know of a better way, write me so I can look into it, but first, send me your Restoration Testimony.

Write me when you're done so I can attach the link to your testimony for our members to donate and also so that I move it ahead of the other restored marriages that are in line to come up.

Love you lots!

~ *Erin*

We were able to send Vicky enough money for about SIX months average income for Kenya! Praise the Lord—now here is her testimony!!

"My Testimony"

My problems began when I started suspecting my husband was in adultery. I was not sure but he had changed. So like all women do I started going through his stuff to see what I could find. One day he came home drunk and I managed to get hold of his cell phone. That's where I found the truth. My whole world came crashing down. I didn't know what to do. I talked to my friends who, as usual, told me to confront him, and I was a fool and did whatever I was told by someone who didn't know what the right thing was to do.

I confronted him and that's when all hell broke loose. He told me he was seeing this woman and no one or anything would stop him because she was pregnant with his child. I didn't stop there. I then foolishly went and told his parents but nothing changed.

My situation got worse. He moved out and started living with OW. He told me I could tell whoever I wanted but no one would help me. That's when I came to my senses and remembered that actually there was Someone I could tell and He would help. I turned to God and asked Him for help.

I started reading the Bible and praying for God's guidance. I felt at peace in my heart though it was broken. One day I was on a bus going home from work and there was this lady holding some papers. The heading was praying scriptures for your marriage. I got eager of know what it was and the next day I went to the Internet and Googled the heading. I found so many websites about marriage restoration.

That is where I found YOU! I found out about the RYM book. I read the book and even before I could finish the first chapter I saw what kind of a wife I was. I knelt down before the computer and asked God to forgive me and asked Him to give me another chance in my marriage. I started applying the principles in the book and I felt that the time was coming for my victory. I didn't care whether the OW was pregnant or not but I knew my victory would come in handy. I used to pray and cry, but this time, I was crying to my God for His mercies.

One month had passed since my husband moved out. He used to come home while I was at work to see the children but all this while I had not seen or talked to him because he told me not to call him. I obeyed like the RYM book says. I kept telling God that I needed to see my husband so he could see the changes in me.

One Sunday morning God remembered me. I received a call from my husband. He wanted to know if I was at home because he wanted to come and pick some of his stuff from the house. I started praising God for I knew it was His plan. I knew it was His plan because my husband would always come in the house during the day and pick whatever he wanted when we weren't home, but this time he wanted to come while I was at home. PTL!

The reason he came however was because he had lost his job. He wanted me to loan him some money (which I did because as you taught us, we were still married and that is being submissive). That day we talked and had fun, enough that he didn't end up taking anything with him! When he lost his job, it was the beginning of his troubles with the OW, and the beginning of my victory!

The OW I am sad to say had abortion. I later found that she got pregnant so that my husband would marry her and so all his money would be hers, but now he didn't have a job so, no money. She became sharp like the book of Proverbs 5:3-5 says. They began fighting and my husband would come over to see me. One time she hit him with a stool and broke his hand. He came over and lied that he had fallen down while on the bus. That's when he realized she was after his money and there was no love.

He was ashamed of coming back to my house completely so he rented another flat where he lived alone. He told my cousin that he had said a lot of hurtful words to me and he felt embarrassed. He said I was treating him well, but he had hurt me enough, and everything I and his family had warned him of, had come to pass.

He asked my cousin for advise and she told him to do what the prodigal son did but he couldn't. He thought if he came back I would laugh at him because I had won.

He stayed alone for quite sometime, but because he didn't have a job the burden of paying his and my rent became too big. God turned his heart and he finally decided he needed to move back with me and kids!

He called all his family members and asked them to forgive him and he accepted his mistakes. He told them he had learned his lesson and he was starting all over again... if I was ready to accept and forgive him. He wanted us to be a family again. I told him I had forgiven him and I asked him to forgive me too for I was contentious and I was not a good wife to him; we were given his parents blessing!

It hasn't been easy since God restored my marriage. It is not easy because the devil always reminds me of all the pain my husband caused me, but I have learned to overcome him with time with the Lord and my prayers.

My husband and I have become true friends. He began to tell me all his troubles and his plans, which he never did before. When I am not in the house and he wants to go somewhere, he calls or writes a note so I can know where he is and I do the same.

It is not always smooth but I am sure that good times are ahead. Even after I lost my job I have something to thank God for—my family is together and complete!

I have learned to be content with what I have and am trusting God because He promised He will supply my needs according to His riches in glory through Christ Jesus (Phil. 4:19). Also, knowing He is my Shepherd, I shall not lack (Psalm 23:1).

I thank God for fighting on my behalf. There are so many things He did for me behind the scenes. I thought my husband was happy with OW but I hear he had been regretting everything he had done from the beginning, especially after God said it was time for him to see the changes in me.

God is faithful to those who wait. Ladies, wait patiently on the Lord for He is true to His promises. He will answer your prayers when the time is right. It might seem long, but He will eventually hear your prayers.

Thank Erin also for her ministry. God bless you for using you to show us the truth. I thought I was a perfect wife but I was wrong. I have learned to listen more than talking and I am submissive. Erin, may the Almighty God reward you for your great ministry.

Ladies always look at Jesus and not the water when He asks you to get out of the boat. Because, if you look at the water you will sink but, if you look at Jesus you will walk on the water!!

God bless you all. AMEN!

~ Vicky in Kenya, Africa, RESTORED

Chapter 18

Charlotte

"A broken and a contrite heart,
O God, You will not despise."
— Psalm 51:17

"Screaming Matches Stop"

My husband and I had a troubled relationship. There were always screaming matches if I did not get my own way.

In December, I found out that my husband was seeing another woman. Desperate to save my marriage, I placed many prayer requests on different websites, hoping that God would save my marriage. It was not long afterwards that I received an email from a lady named Hilary encouraging me, and asking if I was willing to follow God's principles to save my marriage. Hilary sent me the book "How God can and will restore your marriage." When I began reading the book, I realised how much I was doing wrong in my marriage.

In February 2004, my husband moved out to be with the other woman. Please remember I was not a Christian before this. When my husband moved out, I had no one, only my Lord. I had asked Hilary if she would be my encouragement partner and she agreed, but I changed jobs and lost contact with her. I could not ask my friends to pray with me because they did not believe in God. Erin's book and the Lord kept me sane. I began reading and praying in ways that I never did before. Psalm 23 became my salvation.

The first thing God taught me was to **stop talking about my situation.** He then taught me to listen and be humble. The Lord was so good to me, He showed me all my faults and what I had done wrong in my marriage. He taught me how to be a biblical wife.

My husband and I had **no contact** when he left—we would see each other on the street and it was as if we were strangers. One day, I received a call from my husband asking for my mom's number so that he could speak to our daughter. I thanked him for remembering our daughter, and gave him her telephone number. Soon afterwards, he began to call whenever he needed something. We slowly became friends again.

Through Erin's books and the Bible, I learnt to put my tears in a bottle. I learnt to trust the Lord to take over my problems and situation. As hard as it was, I learned **not** to call my husband.

I remember a rainy Saturday when my husband came through and he started to dismantle the bedroom set to take it with him and I asked him how could he take something we had bought together to live with the OW. Then and there, he broke the furniture and left. I remember asking the Lord, "Now what?" Instead of ranting and raving, I got on my knees and prayed to the Lord for help. My Saviour gave me peace that day and showed me that He was there to carry me even through the mistake that I had made by saying something like that and trying to stop my husband.

There was not really a turning point I think because my restoration was all so unexpected. My husband and I did not really see each other at all. I avoided him whenever I could because I was scared of hearing him tell me that I was desperate to have him back. The last time we had spoken, he had made it very clear that he was **in love with the OW** and that he **would not return**, but we should just remain friends.

Then last Thursday, when I was at work, I received a call from the downstairs reception saying that there was a gentleman at the reception to see me. When I went to see who his gentleman was, I saw it was my husband! He told me that he had lost everything and wanted to work at his marriage. He had no place to stay and could he please come back home?

My husband brought all of his things home and I am so thankful to the Lord for restoring my marriage. We still have a very long way to go but I know that the Lord will not let me down as long as I keep doing everything the same and allowing Him to finish what He started.

I know that God can move mountains, and nothing happens in **my** timing but in His timing!

~ Charlotte in South Africa, RESTORED!!

Chapter 19

Linda

"A broken and a contrite heart,
O God, You will not despise."
— Psalm 51:17

"Not Just a Fairy Tale"

RMI, I had to write to thank you so very much for your birthday gift. I had not been on your site for a while due to so many things going on in my life, and one of those being that I'm now restored to my husband!! I apologize for never submitting a testimony but wanted to thank you because I have moved back to where he is this last December. We've been back together since that time, give or take a few months.

I came to see my husband when he asked me to visit, it took him a bit to make up his mind about our future, but I knew it would happen in His timing. A few months later, we were making plans for me to move to be with him.

If there are typos please forgive me. I had eye surgery recently and can't see too well currently. The Lord is faithful in all things, He has shown me this many times over the past few years, and thanks to what you taught me, I understood how everything happens for a reason.

My thoughts and prayers go out to those who are still in waiting for restoration and I want to thank you, your partners and all the ministers for caring enough for us that you devote yourself to His work and sharing His love with those of us who are hurting and who everyone else is misguiding.
So, please let everyone know, if you follow and trust what you say in your books and lessons—restoration does happen. It's not a fairy tale or wishful thinking ... God wants us to be with the love of our youth,

as well as with HIM once we become His bride. GOD restores. God Bless you all!!

~ Linda in Illinois

"God is Absolutely AMAZING!!!!!"

I joined RMI in June and told my sister-in-law about it. She joined in November. It had been three years since her husband had lived with the OW as well as had a child with her.

We began to pray a hedge of thorns around the OW as well as fasting, binding and loosing, even though there were numerous attempts by her husband to go ahead with the divorce.

On Thursday, we fasted and prayed a hedge of thorns around the OW. That day, her husband came home to his wife at 3 a.m. in the morning, throwing up everywhere. He confessed and apologized for everything. He said that he had made a terrible mistake and wanted to come back home! Only God can do this! It is complete—he does not want to have anything to do with the OW! God is so good! He said that they had begun to fight and quarrel all the time!

Please be quiet and pray and fast. Ask God to send confusion into that relationship and pray a hedge of thorns over the OW, and bind your husband's flesh to the will of God. God is so awesome! No counselor, no friend, no pastor can restore—only our Heavenly Father can restore! Amen!

Please be meek and quiet, because when God sends trouble, your husband will come home looking for peace!!!!

~ Lisa in Canada

Chapter 20

Tracy

"A broken and a contrite heart,
O God, You will not despise."
— Psalm 51:17

"The Lord Changed Me!!"

I will never forget November 11. That was the day my life was changed forever. My husband and I split up after nine years of marriage. I was six months pregnant and used my "condition" as an excuse to torment my husband emotionally by nagging him and being a very contentious woman.

Now that I have been "through the fire", let me tell you what the Lord can do—He changed me!!! I was a liar and an adulteress. It took my family being separated and my house being torn down by my own destructive hands, for the Lord to get my attention. I was so desperate to find answers for "what the devil took away from me". But the devil did not steal anything—I gave it to him!

I was searching another Christian site and there was a reference to RMI—that was when the Lord began to heal me. Erin, I can't thank you enough for helping me through this ordeal!

God, through Jesus Christ, changed me and stripped me of all the things I was hiding behind. I hid behind the lies I told everyone: what a terrible man my husband was, how he abandoned me when I was six months pregnant with his child. But when I got a hold of RMI and began using the biblical principles and verses that Erin wrote in the book, it made me repent. I had to go back to the same people I had lied to and tell them the truth—I threw my husband out.

I was a very prideful woman who always "loved" the Lord. But I was not willing to obey what the Lord was saying to me. I am considered "gifted" and the Lord has always guided my life. But if the Lord told me to do something, I would not do it. I would even lie to Him and say "Lord, I will obey" but He knew my heart and He knew I was lying before I even uttered the words!

Now, I know better and some of the Scriptures that helped me were "faith without works is dead", and "it is impossible to please God without faith". After I learnt this, when the Lord told me to do something (such as to stop lying and tell the truth), I obeyed immediately.

I sought answers from the RMI books and website, and also from Scriptures. When the opportunity came for me to be loving to my husband, I obeyed and the hate wall immediately fell down! I could not believe it!! Let me also add that when I did not obey the Lord, my husband fell deeper and deeper into adultery. He eventually moved in with a married woman and lived with her for four years!!

Ladies, I am telling you to obey the Lord, be anxious for nothing and hold fast to your faith! I am not just telling you what I heard, I am telling you what I lived! The Word of God is alive!!! My husband has

now been home for three weeks! I know that the OW is calling his cell-phone, but my trust is in the Lord who has removed her.

I pray everyday that she finds peace and her marriage is also restored. I have a calling on my life—I believe I am being led to ministry. I do

not know how or when the Lord is going to use me, but I am waiting to hear from Him.

Be blessed! May the work of God sustain you, my sisters and brothers!

Erin may the Lord bless you continually for all the marriages you have saved!

~ Tracy in Louisian

"Be Still and Know that He is God!"

My husband and I where going through a terrible separation because of adultery. We were separated for five months.

Now we are back together because the Word of God teaches us to forgive and now we are stronger in our relationship with God and each other.

Forgiveness is one of the keys to every lasting relationship.

We are back together due to a lot of fasting and praying, which is the main key.

Marriages that are going through separation: BE STILL AND KNOW THAT HE IS GOD AND HE WILL DO WHAT HE SAID HE WILL DO JUST KEEP FASTING, PRAYING AND BELIEVING AND HE WILL COME THROUGH.

GOD BLESS!

Chapter 21

Magenta

"A broken and a contrite heart,
O God, You will not despise."
— Psalm 51:17

"Praying Together"

I have been married for 13 years. My life was shaken when my husband asked me what I would do without him. I knew of no known illness he had that would permeate this question. I knew we had disagreements about parenting my stepsons: I was a disciplinarian but my husband had his own method. To me his method allowed the boys to divide us against each other. I saw the problem, but my husband did not want to come in prayer with this situation.

The situation got out of hand. The boys' lives became a burden to us. They were rebellious, disobedient and disrespectful to anyone that tried to bring order in their lives. I went to God in prayer and asked Him for guidance. We distanced ourselves while still living in the same house.

My husband slept down the hall and I slept in our room. This was a very difficult period. My husband was stubborn, but God was still working. I was even more stubborn, but God was still working on me even more. My husband lost a lot of weight over stressing about his future. Thankfully I continued to stay where God wanted me to stay, because I have been through some valleys and I knew that God was my only strength and my salvation, and I was not going to allow fear to enter my heart to what looked like the inevitable.

Then my husband began reading the Word and praying more, praying with me! I began asking God to help me to continue to pray alone, by myself, and not to only pray when we prayed together. Then without me saying anything, my husband began to pray for the boys (17 & 18) to be accountable for their actions and come to know God personally. Because they are choosing the things of the world and my husband continues to try to save them, I have been quiet and respectful, and instead my prayers are simply that he would release them totally in the hands of God and believe that God is sovereign, knowing He can do whatever He wants to do. But this is my husband's issue and not mine.

Even though I didn't know my husband’s heart because he was consumed with the boys, I did believe he loved me and I wanted his complete love and not share it with anyone. I believed that he would realize that he cannot live his life for his kids, but to realize the order that God set up for man is to put me first. I prayed that one day my husband would realize how much I love him and that I would be first.

Then I realized that I had missed the most important relationship of all and that is why I longed for what was second-rate. He is Who we need and where our focus needs to be!

The more I came to know and want Him, the more He taught me to put my trust in Him, not to lean to my own understanding. To acknowledge Him and He will direct my path, to not fret, to commit my ways unto Him, to delight in Him, to rest in Him and to wait on Him. To make HIM first, and to stop being jealous of my husband's relationship and concern for our boys, when I had continually been unfaithful to my Husband!

He then began to help me to forgive and to release all my cares to Him. Then I was able to bear anything and everything when the water got rough. I knew that He and His Word was comfort to my soul. He gave me a peace that surpasses all understanding and my view of my world changed completely.

The principles God taught me were: staying with the Lord and putting Him first, praying, seeking Him and no one else, letting the words of my mouth and the meditation of my heart to be acceptable to Him, helping others in spite of my situation and presenting my body as a living sacrifice to Him because He deserved all of me.

As much as I prayed, I struggled with keeping my eyes on the Lord. Sometimes, the weight of the burden seemed to hard to bear. I did not want to be in this situation at this time in my life. I had been through so much, but He was always there to help me by reminding me that He was my comfort and strength and that He loved me in spite of others. He cradled me with His love and I became His bride.

Then one day the Lord said something I wasn't sure was Him. He said to go and talk to your husband, ask him what he wanted to do. Did he want out of this marriage? I thought it may be the enemy, but I felt it was His voice I was hearing. So after work that day I stopped and bought a nice meal and set the table. We sat down to eat and I began the conversation, inside asking the Lord to stop me if it was a trap. I asked him, "Do you want to stay in this marriage?" And he said yes, and thanked me for giving him the choice to leave if he wanted to because he'd felt trapped. So I then told him that full forgiveness had taken place at that moment, and he said we had to confess our sins and ask God to forgive both of us and to forgive one another. We did just that, then agreed in the name of Jesus, and from that moment on He took hold of our marriage.

He restored our marriage completely! And I give Him ALL the praise. Together we are continuing to seek Him and ask Him for His guidance and to continue to help us with the boys. Satan continues to have a foothold on them but we know God's light illuminates our hearts and He is keeping us praying, and that's what the boys need, a marriage united with Him being first! Sometimes I feel like I would like a little more closeness with my husband, but I know God is working that out too. For now I need to give him his space to find His closeness with the Lord, so he has the love to give me.

Thank you RMI for changing our lives!!

~ Magenta in California

Chapter 22

Jen

"A broken and a contrite heart,
O God, You will not despise."
— Psalm 51:17

"A Clear Vision!"

Job 33:14-18 says, "For God does speak-now one way, now another-though man may not perceive it. In a dream, in a vision of the night, when deep sleep falls on men as they slumber in their beds, he may speak in their ears and terrify them with warnings, to turn man from wrongdoing and keep him from pride, to preserve his soul from the pit, his life from perishing by the sword."

My husband first contacted me in August after he left in May more than 3 years ago! Right before he called, I highlighted and dated this scripture above and just a few days short before the New Year, His promise to me has come to pass!!

My future husband called and told me that he woke up with such a clear vision of me sitting beside him, telling him that he needed to call me. He said that he woke up and even walked around, and it was still as clear as could be.

Since that night, he has told me he wants to start working on things and that he no longer (or really ever) thinks of me as his ex-wife! He told me he would like to see me again, and to please come back to the state that he's in for a visit so we can begin getting things back together! (I haven't seen him since he left, we live several states apart.)

Several other concerns and prayers were answered for me throughout our talks. He told me I didn't have to refinance the house to put it in my name because he thinks we should probably put it up for sale by the end of the year! I have been praying about this because I couldn't afford to pay those fees, and most likely wouldn't qualify for the payment. He stated that he is open to remarriage, but would like to "see changes in me" first!

He said that once we remarry he would like to look for another house back in Michigan! (I just started praying for favor to go back there. My rebellion caused us to move to Missouri, and eventually lead to the destruction of my marriage.)

He also told me he will never use an attorney again because of all of the wrong and hurtful information he received!! Thank goodness I didn't get an attorney and cause more pain for him!

Many more praises could be given. The Lord really has passed on so many blessings, and in all of this, paid attention to every detail!

~ Jen in Missouri

"He's Going Back Home!"

I've known my friend for many years, since middle school. We both got married around the same time. He's 28 and decided that after 4 years of marriage he didn't want to continue his marriage.

He and his wife had been having problems and instead of working out the situations he was deceived by Satan. He would talk to me sometimes and I would tell him not to give up trying to work things out. I didn't think that he was taking my advice until one day out of nowhere he came up to me very happy telling me that he was going back home and he appreciated the advice that I was giving him!

The day before that, he was in a taxicab and the cab driver just so happened to be a pastor. He told me that the pastor started telling him about his situation not even knowing him. He also said he felt that was God talking to him through the pastor and he was going to obey God!

He gave up the other women and told her he was going back home! I was so happy for him and his wife who is expecting another child.

~ Cathy in Michigan

"God Fixed It!"

Before RMI I didn't know "how" to be a wife. Married for 6 years, I let negative thoughts rule my mind. Instead of "letting go and letting God", I wanted to fix things myself. And you can't fix it yourself. You have to step yourself out of your situation and let God totally fix it Himself.

To not think negatively is how I was changed, to remove myself and allow God to do His will. My husband and I got back together the week after Christmas, after being separated for a month. Not long after, we found out I was pregnant! We just had our third daughter this past June, we praise God! God is Awesome!

The principles God taught me were to think outside the "what about me" box. To be what I should be, and not what I was. The turning point of my restoration was letting God ... We have to put our worries on Him, and do it. We can't just say it, we have to do it. We have to give Him all of our burdens.

God gave us another baby... :) And a happier, healthier marriage!

~ *Melissa in Texas*

"God was Always There!"

My husband has been home for two weeks and says he is "happy" with me! I feel happy too.

It has almost been three years since the break up, but there were troubles through our fifteen years of marriage.

I wanted to be married so bad that I walked into a situation unknowingly, falling for a separated man. My optimism was dashed over and over with the problems of this involvement, but I didn't understand why.

Once I had worked through the RMI materials, reading them over and over, I had a chance to put them to practice since we stayed in touch. There were still long gaps in our progress.

In the middle of our struggles, how mind boggled I was and how not knowing. No matter how I used my own understanding, I got nowhere. I came more and more to understand my Queen Esther destiny, and stuck to it.

God was always there. My Lord Jesus always looked on me with His compassion. The Word was my lifeboat! I learned to see with different eyes!

I don't know what is in store but I keep my eyes on Him.

Thanks to RMI, my ePartners, my home fellowship partner, and the praise reports! Pray that this will always be a happy marriage, as God's will.

~ *Karen in North Carolina*

Chapter 23

Cynthia

"A broken and a contrite heart,
O God, You will not despise."

— Psalm 51:17

"Sheeps Clothing"

We were married fifteen years and I was miserable because of my husband's irresponsible financial habits and believing he was placing his family before me. The bitterness grew in me over the years and I finally thought I had enough. He attended church but I did not. Then I met a man. I was blinded and could not see the trap set for me and what this would do to my family. This led to a divorce and the divorce then led me to seek God.

I began to attend T.D. Jake's Church - Potter's House here in Dallas, which was recommended by my best friend because she explained that this church teaches about women issues. She was right. I began to learn the tricks of Satan. He knew my weakness and feelings of lack of attention from my husband. This "new" man was a wolf in sheep's clothing—always giving me compliments (something my husband never did). He dressed and appeared very professional and responsible. Thankfully God never left me as He tells us in His Word during this time.

I began to pray for my marriage and stand on His promises of restoration I found by coming to RMI. It was a battle because during this time span of over a year my husband left the church and went into the world due to being so hurt by what I'd done. I hungered for the Word and began to read the Bible and different books about spiritual warfare.

I learned that we live by faith, not by sight. If anyone would have seen how bad things were between my husband and I, they would never believe how we are today!! We are now attending church together with our two sons. The LORD taught me to be still and know that He is God because I am a control freak and I try to fix everything myself, which led to more issues that made things worse.

There were nights that I cried out because I felt desperate, sometimes suicidal thoughts would enter my mind but then I would sense my Heavenly Husband next to me, and I would suddenly feel this peace come over my entire body and I would calm down. I had so many questions and when I would turn on the TV or radio, open a book or hear from a friend, the answer would come, very specific to my question at the time which was His way of speaking to me.

I was scheduled to go to court for the divorce and my mother-in-law was praying that the "doors to the case be shut." I still went out of anger towards my husband. But even with the wrong attitude, He was faithful and did the impossible. First the judge was not there, she was out of town and no one told us. Second, my name was not on the new docket of cases to be heard that day. Third, my lawyer came in saying, "We have a problem." The court stamped the wrong Child Support case on the forms. Fourth, the replacement judge we found said, "I won't touch that," because the paperwork was not in order.

We finally found a judge to swear me in but when it was over my lawyer and I stopped and sat down. I asked him, "I'm confused, am I divorced or not?" He said, "Put it this way, I would not run off and get married!" Out of a courthouse full of people that went for a divorce; I left there still married! God finally did allow the divorce to go through several months later due to the hardness of my heart because that is what I needed and He knew it.

The turning point, in the end, was when I finally stopped trying to fix the situation myself and stopped trying to make my husband do what I said and wanted. I finally and completely let it go, which is what RMI says to do but so few of us do it, we tell ourselves and try to convince others but until we do, things keep getting worse. This gave me time to just concentrate on learning the Word, getting closer to my HH and that's when things finally began to change permanently. I had peace and I would simply ask God to give my husband a new heart because by this time his heart was hardened completely towards me. Yet after only a couple of months, he started coming over to our house, first to fix things around the house here and there, and then staying longer all with me not having to try to make it happen.

My mother-in-law would tell me to ASK God to restore my marriage but I was stubborn at times and I would say, "God knows my heart." She said to ask Him when He would restore my marriage, so I finally let my pride go and did it as she asked. That night I had a dream, mind you it was that very same night. It was about a date on a calendar. It was only a couple of weeks from that night and I thought surely it would take God a couple of years not weeks. But it did happen! And though there was still a spiritual battle after he came home, which again RMI tells us will happen and why we need to make sure where our loyalty lies, with Him, it was still difficult. It took almost a year or more of God creating a new heart in my husband, that hardened towards me for good reason, and also for me to see the things that He still needed to change in me.

Believe it or not, this year we will celebrate our 20th anniversary and it's been a full five years of restoration, and things just keep getting better and better!! I continuing to put Him first, go to Him to fix everything and spend a lot of time in His Word daily, reading my Bible as my daily map. I now attend a women’s prayer group in my area, praying for restored marriages and lives to be changed as He's changed mine. And my husband also attends his own prayer meetings and Bible studies. Now I know that I have to stay in the Word; I want to stay in the Word in order to keep my mind renewed, refreshed and on the right track!!

~ Cynthia in Texas, Restored!!!

Chapter 24

Axel

"A broken and a contrite heart,
O God, You will not despise."

— Psalm 51:17

"Who am I?"

The 1st Key to Restoration-"Who am I?"

"Just a man," I keep reminding myself. I am unable to control anything it would seem.

I look up and cry out "why?!"

No answer.

Does He hear what we say?

Does my pain, the pain in my heart, somehow matter enough to Him that He could take it away?

Why doesn't He answer in the way that I want, WHEN I want?

I had lost what was most valuable to me: My wife and son. She wanted nothing to do with me.

When I was able to see my son it was though I was reduced to more of a relative than his father.

So much pain.

I knew what the Bible said. I had read through it more then once growing up in a Christian home. Certain scriptures would come to mind and give me hope. Hope was almost gone though.

One day it left altogether.

I had reached bottom and knew it. I knew God was "there." I had seen Him in the lives that He changed. In the miracles that He did every day. It takes more faith to look around at the wonders of our world and say that it made ITSELF. No, I never doubted his EXISTENCE, only his PLAN.

I felt at times that I was not IN IT... That somehow everyone else around me had it better.. They had the blessings and I didn't. Their prayers were being heard- while mine were being shoved onto some holy "filing cabinet," never to see the light of day.

I would love to tell you that my breakthrough happened right then. That my life turned around in a moment and God just delivered me in the most miraculous way.

But it didn't happen that way.

Months went by and I kept moving on. But not in a good way... My faith was shaken... My heart that was once broken became a hard, crusted-over brick in my chest. Not able to give out a tender 'God breathed' love or even receive it. The scar tissue had become almost impenetrable. I vowed I would never hurt like that again.

God had allowed everything to be taken from me. My family, my job, my "stuff"- all replaced with self-loathing and despair. Some days I wanted no more of this life. I didn't want to wake up to "this" in the morning. To know that I had to live in this feeling of being unloved. Forgotten.

-But one day... There was a change-

God gave forgiveness. He gave love. He gave it all so long ago. I had forgotten what His son had done for all of us. If His blood could save us from all the sins that we would EVER commit - why couldn't that same blood cover my life? My marriage? My family?

"Take heart, have faith for I have overcome the world.""In the world you have tribulation, but take courage; I have overcome the world." John 16:33

I was ready to try once more. Even if the outcome was to live a SINGLE life for Jesus- I wanted that. Did I want my wife back? Sure! My son? Of course... Did I have the faith to believe that it would happen? Wish that I could say I did, but I really didn't. I just knew that God COULD do all things. He WOULD be good and faithful in all things like His word said.

—I needed to be faithful to HIM as well—

I had stopped being faithful. I had always remembered to ask God for what I needed when I needed it—But what about remembering to give BACK to HIM? You may say, "Well God doesn't need anything. He's GOD. He made it ALL."While in a way this is true, this line of thinking is damaging and does not line up with the words He gave us to live by in scripture.

"Bring the whole tithe into the storehouse, so that there may be food in My house, and **test Me now** in this," says the Lord of hosts, "if I will not open for you the windows of heaven and pour out for you a blessing until it overflows. Then I will rebuke the devourer for you, so that it will not destroy the fruits of the ground; nor will your vine in the field cast its grapes," says the Lord of hosts. "All the nations will call you blessed, for you shall be a delightful land," says the Lord of hosts. Malachi 3:10-12

He said TEST me - The ONLY place in the bible where He tells us to do that.

You're probably asking, "What does GIVING have to do with restoring my marriage??"

More then you know.

He told us to be faithful in **all** things. Not just some things.

So how can He bless, restore and give to us what we need and desire when we literally have His hands bound with spiritual "handcuffs"?? The answer is: He can't. We are limiting Him and His working in our lives. And the tragedy is, we don't even know it.

-What IS Tithing??

Tithing, as you read above, is giving God's portion of our income BACK to Him. What is His portion? His word tells us that 10% belongs to Him. That is all He asks. You may say, "I can't AFFORD to tithe."

I am here to tell you that you can't afford NOT to! It cost me everything, literally everything by stealing from God.

Malachi 3:7-9 explains what I did and what most of you are doing too.

"From the days of your fathers you have turned aside from My statutes and have not kept them. Return to Me, and I will return to you," says the Lord of hosts. "But you say, 'How shall we return?' Will a man rob God? Yet you are robbing Me! But you say, 'How have we robbed You?' In tithes and offerings. You are cursed with a curse, for you are robbing Me, the whole nation of you!

Ignore or dismiss His word and suffer the consequences. OR TEST God, just as He asked you to do and see how He will do MORE with 10% than YOU can do with the other 90% and how this will slam the door on the devourer who has stolen your life from you.

Where does my tithe belong?

Your tithe belongs where you are being spiritually "fed."

It could be your home church. It could be this ministry. Wherever that place is be FAITHFUL and give back to Him. I promise you will see big changes take place in your life.

I did in mine.

When I started to give that 10% of what I had (which, being without a job was very little and took all of my faith) to this ministry, I starting to see things happen. Breakthroughs started to take place. It was a journey that started with God showing me this simple truth: You can't out give God and it's foolish to steal from Him.

Jumping to the "good part" of my story... **Yes, my marriage was restored.** Yes, my wife and I are in love and are better people now. Yes, I am able to see my son everyday and I even know what his favorite cereal is!!

These gifts I am so thankful for!

I will never forget what started this chain-reaction of events and blessings. An easily, overlooked command. To "give and it shall be given." To entrust all "worldly wealth" to Him. So that He can show you things that are more precious than handfuls of diamonds or bars of pure gold.

I am a rich man.

Not in earthly wealth, but in riches that will last forever.

-Axel Thiele

Axel's Update:

"Does Restoration really Stick?"

I'm Many wonder if restoration sticks—so I am here today to let you know I've been restored and living "happily ever after" with my wife Kasey for more than 4 glorious years! God restored my marriage slowly but surely from the day I first stopped **robbing God.** My wife & I remarried New Year's Eve.

And that's not all, since our restoration the Lord has blessed us with a second son, a boy who looks like my beautiful wife. Today we are more in love than ever, no longer stealing from God, and enormously blessed—far beyond what we deserve.

Just this year my wife and I felt called to move away from family to help plant a church. Soon after we arrived, the job that we believed would support our family didn't work out. Seeking God, we sold just about everything while He opened the door to allow me to do something I've loved since I was a small boy—using my hands and building things.

With my love and God-given talent for working with wood, along with my wife's amazing eye for design, I began making and selling reclaimed wood products.

I identify with reclaimed wood because He reclaimed me and took my life that no longer had a purpose (after loosing my wife and son after our divorce)—but HE made my life new again with a purpose!

When I go looking for wood that's been thrown away, I can't help but think of how we men need to look for other men who have been thrown away by their wives, families, communities, churches and friends due to their marriage falling apart. Let's rejoice because WITH God their lives can change just as mine did and continues to do!

Matthew 19:26—

And looking at them Jesus said to them, "With people this is impossible, but with God all things are possible."

Mark 10:27—

Looking at them, Jesus said, "With people it is impossible, but not with God ; for all things are possible with God."

Luke 1:37—

"For nothing will be impossible with God."

Luke 18:27—

But He said, "The things that are impossible with people are possible with God."

And the only way to be WITH GOD is to:

Psalm 37:4—

"Delight yourself in the Lord and He will give you the desires of your heart."

Isaiah 30:18—

"Therefore the LORD longs to be gracious to you, and therefore He waits on high to have compassion on you. For the LORD is a God of justice; how blessed are all those **who long for Him."**

Turn from everything that's wrong in your life and:

Matthew 6:33—

"seek first His kingdom and His righteousness, and all these things shall be added to you."

Then, due to His love and mercy:

Isaiah 61:7-8—

"Instead of your shame you will have a DOUBLE portion, and instead of humiliation they will shout for joy over their portion Therefore they will possess a DOUBLE portion in their land, Everlasting joy will be theirs. For I, the LORD, love justice, I hate robbery . . . And I will faithfully give them their recompense And make an everlasting covenant with them."

Romans 8:28—

"And we know that God causes all things to work together for good to those who love God, to those who are called according to His purpose."

My wife and I have seen what we went through to work for good.

Genesis 50:20—

"As for you, you meant evil against me, but God meant it for good in order to bring about this present result, to preserve many people alive."

We hope you will spread the word that turning to HIM and making HIM the center of your life will change EVERYTHING!

Esther 4:14—

"For if you remain silent at this time, relief and deliverance will arise for the Jews from another place and you and your father's house will perish. And who knows whether you have not attained royalty for such a time as this?"

And though many situations and people may come against you, remember:

1 Peter 3:13-15—

"Who is there to harm you if you prove zealous for what is good? But even if you should suffer for the sake of righteousness, you are blessed and do not fear their intimidation, and do not be troubled, but sanctify Christ as Lord in your hearts, always being ready to make a defense to everyone who asks you to give an account for the hope that is in you, yet with gentleness and reverence."

Update: Axel is Erin Thiele's son and has been restored since 2009. He and His wife Kasey also added a restoration baby to their family, a second son born a year later. Everyone notices their strong and "extremely loving" marriage reflected too in the amazing sons they are raising for the Lord.

Chapter 25

Chizette

"A broken and a contrite heart,
O God, You will not despise."

— Psalm 51:17

"Restored Better than Before!!"

I'm submitting this for my precious best friend because she does not have computer access. She and her husband had been separated for 3 years —and she had no clue her husband was leaving, he just left. So I gave her the RYM Book and the WW for us to study together.

Needless to say she was devastated, crushed, and brokenhearted! She went numb. The enemy lied to her telling her she wasn't worth loving. No one would ever love her. Not to mention she was way too old for her very young husband, over 15 years difference.

Well God is no respecter of race, age, of persons! God had plans for these precious people of His!

My friend turned all her being to the lord. She sought people to "love on" because in her brain it helped her get her mind off her broken (unworthy to be loved) heart. She started ministering in addiction recovery classes in her church because she'd turned to food to help ease her pain as well. Three long years of not hearing from her husband for months on end, then she hit bottom and everyone pressured her into filing for divorce.

My friend went to her husband to get his signature, but God had other plans. Her husband was going to sign it because he thought he had to (being as he was so young he didn't know what was going on, other then he was out in the world), but the notary couldn't accept his signature—he wasn't allowed to sign because his driver's license was not valid!! God made it impossible for signing of any divorce papers!

So they once again went about their separate lives, then finally, one night, he hit bottom in the drug scene—praise the Lord for bringing him to himself! Praise the Lord for using that whole horrible drug world (Satan means for destruction and God used it for his glory!) That night he called home and told his wife he couldn't handle that kind of life anymore. When we heard, we prayed huge warfare for him that night; for God to remove him from that world. The next day he called her and said his grandpa was dying and he had to go to Arizona! God took him out of that world in less than 24 hours!

My friend was miserable saying she didn't mean for God to move him out of the state, but God moved him to where he had to get a job to be able to stay with his grandparents. And his grandparents are God fearing—it was the best place God could have moved him!! That's when she pursued the Lord as her Husband more and more. God was healing her so she could be the Godly wife He called her to be and what her husband would need.

When she was ready is when God finally brought her husband back to Idaho. He kept saying he needed to get a job, but he knew he couldn't because he couldn't pass any drug tests. God allowed him to become so miserable to the point that he had no food. God's Word says if a man does not work, he does not eat. God's Word says the wicked shall not succeed. He got so miserable, hungry, and sick! Praise the Lord! He was so miserable that one day he cried out to the Lord and was completely set free from the drugs!! No withdrawals at all!!

One day he saw a dump truck driving down the road, so he decided to followed it not knowing why, and he pulled the driver over and asked if they were hiring. The driver said, "Yes, here's a card, get to the office and you'll start Monday." He passed the drug test and he's been working for more than 2 years straight now and is providing for his wife financially (where as before he did not do that). She just told me she has fallen in love all over again due to him being clean from drugs and faithfully working!

With this new man God has blessed her with, my friend can do nothing but praise Him and tell everyone she meets that God can do the impossible! She tells everyone about what happened, and that her husband's body has a new man inside that is totally "loving on" his new Godly wife! They are behaving like newlyweds—all romantic and flirty! God's love is overflowing out of them! God promises He'll restore what the enemy stole from us and better then what it was! They are showing God's promise! Glory be to God!

Thank You Lord for this restored (better than before) marriage and they will serve You, Lord, all the days of their lives together as one! Amen! And thank You for using me to give my friend the truth when she needed you the most. I know in the past I told people the wrong thing, because I was ignorant. Then even when I knew the truth I'd keep it to myself. Thankfully I realized the truth was not mine to hide away, but to share it with everyone in trouble. Thank You for finally helping me to help others!!

~ Chizette in Idaho

"Just Married!"

Praise God! My marriage was restored!!! We were legally married again after three and a half years of divorce! I never saw him, didn't know where he was, but this ministry told me none of that mattered if I just made the Lord my Husband.

Praise the Mighty name of Jesus Christ my Heavenly Husband. All praise and glory belong to Him and as RMI says, Nothing is impossible with God! Amen and Amen!!!

~ Sharon in California

Chapter 26

Terese

"A broken and a contrite heart,
O God, You will not despise."

— Psalm 51:17

"We ALL Moved Back Home!"

About two and a half years ago I contacted and joined Restore Ministries. I have been believing for the restoration of my marriage and others marriages. I had friends and acquaintances that I stood believing for and other marriages on the prayer list at Restore Ministries. I have seen God move in awesome ways within my situation and also in one of my friend's!

I followed the scriptures outlined in Erin's books. I wrote scriptures on cards and prayed them constantly. I also shared them with others who were hurt because of their own marital situation. As I surrendered my pride over to God and allowed God to humble me, He started making changes in my husband, my children and especially me!

Though at times the changes were painful I am glad we went through them. I have felt a heavy weight was taken off. I didn't realize (until God opened my eyes) I had become that contentious woman and that I was in a bondage that I put myself in by not following God's word as He intended. I was holding on to every word God had been giving me and trusting His word to be true.

One day, my husband came to see me late at night! This was a big surprise, because he normally wouldn't do that. We sat outside talking for hours, then two days later he came back again and told me the ow left him because he would not divorce me or bring our sons to meet her! He was upset about her leaving him and only by the strength and grace of God was I able to sit and listen to him talk about her with out saying a word. My heart felt like it was being ripped out, but I know God held me in His hands.

My husband started coming and spending the weekends with us, but still I was heavy hearted because of the way he felt that night he told me of the other separation. I continued to believe. One of my friends that I was believing for called and told me of how God restored her marriage and thanked me for not giving up on their situation even though she did! This did give me some encouragement.

My husband started staying with us more, but my sons and I were not home. My husband travels a lot with his job and the home we shared was empty most of the time. He would say He was not ready for us to move back in our home. I started being able to go and visit him where he was working! We had beautiful times together. However, he was hesitant because he wasn't sure I would turn back to the person I was in the past.

He was happy with the relationship we were having. We would share our feeling with an openness we never had before. I felt that we were not really totally together until we were all home. This past January we all moved back home! My husband still works out of town a lot and has not yet come to God, but I am believing that it will come to pass in His timing. Thank You Jesus for starting Restore Ministries, for leading me to them and for using them to help guide me through a dark time in my life.

~ Terese in Florida

"Remarried on Saturday"

Hi everyone, guess what? My husband lost his job yesterday—it was the straw that broke the camel's back for him. He is MOVING HOME! I told my husband that I needed to be remarried before he came home and he asked me if I would like to have the ceremony on Monday—my birthday!

Well, we actually are to be remarried in the church on Saturday!! (Since the state paperwork was picked up but the minister was not available till the weekend :o) This is after being divorced for 8 years! Praise the Lord!

~ *Tasha in Bermuda*

"Allowing Him to Be My First Love!"

I was divorced for two years. I had five children--at the time, they were between the ages of 2 to 8 years. During this entire period, the Lord had me stand for my marriage. It was the hardest time of my life and the hardest thing that I have ever had to do, but my marriage has now been restored for three years!!

I would not want to re-live the trials and tribulations of that lesson but I am very grateful to the Lord for His loving mercy and discipline. Truly, the Lord broke my heart through the divorce, but I needed my hard heart broken so that I would allow HIM to become my First Love again.

During this time of purging and learning, the Lord used this ministry to guide and encourage me. The biblical principles instilled through the RMI books and tapes the Lord provided for me are still very valuable today, and I often refer women to the RMI site.

Thank you Erin, for your obedience in sharing the wisdom that the Lord imparted to you through your experiences.

~ *Patricia in Texas*

Chapter 27

Jamie

"A broken and a contrite heart,
O God, You will not despise."

— Psalm 51:17

"Best Friends AGAIN!"

God I dealt with a lot of what is considered "unacceptable" behavior in my marriage. I did not know how to cope with it in the right way! I had to pray for my husband's salvation and deliverance.

I prayed for courage, healing in my situation, and joined many prayer chains. I sowed seeds for my marriage and prayed for my husband to change. But it all began with me learning how to act correctly, and to not REACT! Thank you for your resources, I would share them with anyone! I prayed for others, but I did not have an e-partner. I believe your ministry helps all of us when we all prayed for each other!

I learned that I am still learning, whenever I do go through difficult situation with my husband, I go to prayer and ask God to guide me and to teach me how to treat others. I ask Him to show me how to let go of fear—to let go of my rights and not stand up for myself.

I know I am never alone, God is for me and my marriage and no one can be against me because God moves mountains, and does the impossible! All I can say is, normally I would be yelling, screaming, and reacting negatively; now I love my husband unconditionally—no matter what he says or does! I give him to God.

I also know that God will come through for our marriage, which is faith! He will protect our business, finances, and provide a home for us again.

Thank you so much for your ministry! I learned a lot about healing, forgiving, and not setting boundaries with God --there are no limits with God! I learned how to let go. Most of all I learned to trust in God with all my heart, soul, and mind.

God transformed, renewed, healed, and forgave me so I could forgive my husband! The Lord taught me that God is for us so who CAN be against us? It is my choice to live in happiness or unhappiness, I choose happiness! To do this I must stay focused on the Lord at all times!

He showed my husband and me that we had, and still have, a good life together. This is because the Lord brought us together, and only the Lord can take us apart! We can love each other unconditionally, regardless of the circumstances! I learned to not let people, places and things come between us!

Thank you God for my wonderful marriage! I know You will keep it in Your good will, and Your way! You will work out and move mountains every day to answer our prayers!

Trust in the Lord and He will lead, guide, protect and show us His will at all times! He is healing my husband right now from adultery, (and other things) but most of all, from drinking! I am aware all this time we have been apart is to teach me to trust and lean on the Lord at all times. I have learned how to forgive my husband (and myself).

I do not have to let fear control me, I do not have to allow people, places, or things control me! Bad situations are temporary; faith is believing what is unseen. Restore Ministries really helped me with my healing. To live in the present, let God do the confronting, and not me! Just like in David's prayers, God is in control at all times, God has given us everything we only receive what God has for us in the first place. Seek the Lord's Kingdom, God's Word, walk in it; live in it. There you will find happiness!

Yes, even so, my husband's adultery was very painful for me. I denied it, he denied it, but then the truth came out. I gave it to the Lord, and the Lord is making everything right! He is making sure my husband stays faithful to me right now, (He has already put closure on the OW, and her control and manipulation). Now God is helping my husband to do what is right at all times.

Also, my husband is standing up to the OW! He is seeking to protect himself and OUR marriage! He is also protecting our business, and our assets that the devil has stolen from us. My husband has received the Lord's salvation and deliverance! Because of my healing, I can communicate today and enjoy my husband and he can enjoy his wife! Right now we are learning to grow, change, and live together again as husband and wife!

I was restored when I realized I was doing the same thing over again and expecting different results. It does not work your way; doing it God's way works! My husband realized that he was being used and used emotionally, spiritually, sexually, and financially by the enemy! My husband knew he had a wonderful beautiful wife at home and he was hurting her. He wanted to be responsible and accountable to God and his wife. My husband realized that what he was doing was wrong and sinful, against our marriage, and against his wife, while living in adultery.

Everything was suffering: our marriage, our business, and our home! We have to leave our home because the OW drained us financially, she was out to destroy! (God has intervened though, when we said: "satan we rebuke you against our marriage in the name of Jesus Christ right now!") Now God is in control, no weapons will form against our marriage or my husband! Nothing will be able to stand against us ever again, that is God's promise, our Lord's promise!!

Our restoration really began when we started talking and seeing more of each other, and as I started applying your restoration principles to my spiritual life. Bad doors closed and good doors opened, that's when we started trusting and loving each other unconditionally. Most of all, we live in the present, share beautiful moments, and learn to solve our problems effectively. We focus on the solution with God, not the problem itself!

Instead of fighting, we have peace and great special times together—every experience is a learning experience! We are learning to be best friends again through God. Most of all we are building a wonderful life together! My husband now believes as I do—that what God has put together only God could take apart! Love is kind, patient, understanding, and forgiving!

~ Jamie in Virginia, RESTORED!

"God is so Merciful!"

I was the model of a contentious woman, without even realizing it! When my husband left me, I was completely broken apart. I couldn't eat, sleep, or even function! I searched for advice on the web and found a secular site "Marriage Builders." Even though it was secular, it had a prayer message board and it was through that, that I found Restore Ministries! My life completely changed afterwards; I was given hope. I ordered the book "How God Can and Will Restore Your Marriage" and cried through the entire reading of it. I had done every wrong thing listed not to do in the book since my husband left!

But God is so merciful! I gave myself completely to the Lord, and He started to change me. I applied the principles in the book: I stopped all arguing, I stopped talking to others about my situation, and I let my lawyer go. As a result of this, the hate wall came down! My husband started to call me just to talk!! Then he started taking me out for breakfast, then an occasional lunch, then with our sons for family outings! All this happened while he was still living with the OW!

Then he finally left her and came home, but it did not last. Even though I thought I was ready, I guess I was not! It was much harder applying all the principles 24/7 rather than just on an occasional basis. So he left again, but this time to his own apartment and not to an OW, praise the Lord. This was the most difficult time for me, but it gave me time to grow in the Lord and further refine me—as God wanted me to be refined. I devoted myself to Bible Study, devotionals, church going and singing with praise CD's. I don't think I would have made it without Restore Ministries and Streams in the Desert!

As I said before, God is so merciful! Suddenly and unexpectedly, my husband came back home again this past May. This time I know he is here to stay! We just sold our house that we had lived in for 15 years, and bought a new house. It will be a fresh start without the unpleasant memories of the previous one! It is not easy, but I am so much better prepared for Satan's tricks now. I am a different person and through prayer and the grace of our Lord, I believe wholeheartedly that our marriage is restored for good! Praise the Lord!

~ Carolyn in California, RMI Fellowship Member, RESTORED!!

"Living Proof!"

My marriage has been restored! God has done a tremendous thing in me and in my life. My husband and I have been having problems since we were married. We were both adulterous, had many arguments, etc. I was very contentious and manipulative to everyone; not just my husband! My husband used to say I drove him crazy (which I did) and I drove my husband to the arms of another woman. God then brought me to this website. I bought the book and workbook and eventually God turned my husband's heart back to me!

Things were ok at first, but then I became complacent which gave the enemy free reign to play with my mind and remind me of everything that happened! I became upset and made things worse by committing adultery myself against my husband—which drove him to yet another woman. This time the woman ended up pregnant, and he made plans to stay with this woman and build a family with her.

I let him take our children because I wanted my freedom. I also wanted to be with the OM I was with and I didn't want any distractions! That is how I viewed our children at the time, God had other plans for my alone time though! The Lord got a hold of me this March and did a complete turn around in me. He changed the way I thought acted and lived! He changed my desires from what I wanted to what HE wanted. It got to the point where I did not care if my marriage was restored or not; the only thing I cared about was God's will and what He wanted for me.

I kept praying for His will to be done; not knowing what His will would be. Almost instantly, circumstances began changing in favor of the restoration of my marriage! Like I said earlier, the other woman was pregnant at the time and she ended up having a miscarriage. I didn't know what response to have to that, but I also know God doesn't make mistakes! He is not evil, so I knew when that happened He must not have wanted her to have those children.

Their relationship began deteriorating rapidly and the whole time I was leaning on God! That's a miracle because I don't lean on anyone usually. I used to be the type of woman that wanted to control everything so that's why I say that's a miracle! Then my husband began calling me, and the OW was actually bringing me and my husband closer—without even realizing it through her actions! Eventually my husband began talking everyday with me!

My husband was in a one year lease with this woman, but God miraculously broke the lease! The other woman had to move out of the house and praise the Lord she's out of our life. Praise God He removed the other woman and turned my husband's heart back to me. We also have military housing (my husband is in the Navy) so we don't have to live in the same house they lived in! He found out we had it within a week; which is a miracle because the waiting list for military housing is normally one year! We are really getting a fresh new start!!

Our furniture was stolen by the OW and God made a way for us to get new furniture! She even took the bed that they slept in and left the bed that my daughter used to sleep in, which turns out to be a better bed! She left her treadmill which my husband said I could keep, and she left her 15 cookbooks which he also said I could keep. Things have completely turned around and it is all because of Jesus! The children and I will be moving into our new home in two weeks! Praise the Lord for the miracle He has done with us! God is so good, my situation looked completely hopeless! If someone would have told me in last spring that God was going to restore my marriage, I would have laughed at them! Now I tell everyone that nothing is impossible with God—and I'm living proof!!

~ Vanessa in Florida, RMI Fellowship Member, RESTORED!

Chapter 28

Valerie

"A broken and a contrite heart,
O God, You will not despise."

— Psalm 51:17

"He Used YOU to Change My Life!! "

In a thank you note to our partners, Valerie submitted this:

Dear ladies,

I wanted to let you know that as of two days ago, God has done another miracle. He has restored my marriage, completely unexpectedly. Because of what you have blessed me with, my family has been reunited. Because of what you have blessed me with, Satan lost another battle. Because of what you have blessed me with, I hope to someday raise Christ-like children with my husband. Because of what you have blessed me with, I can bless another woman and hopefully continue the cycle.

You have allowed me to become part of the Lord's revival for marriages and families. I feel truly so blessed that you thought of me, and my broken heart and desperate situation and had compassion on me—and if you're anything like me, you probably didn't have the sufficient funds to really bless someone else, but you did it anyway. And because of that, my life is forever changed by this journey.

So I wish I had more powerful words beyond "thank you." But it's all that I can say—from the bottom of my once-broken heart, thank you! Thank you for allowing the Lord to use you in my life.

After two years of marriage, my husband became ill which led him to be prescribed a certain medication that had a side effect of reckless behavior. That, coupled with my spiritual pride and contentiousness, led to the breakdown of our marriage. My husband asked me to leave the home so he could pursue his dream of basketball. We were separated for six months with absolutely no contact and he filed for divorce two months ago. Two days ago, he called me and dropped the divorce and I moved home…

Lord, I am so humbled by the work you have done in my life and my marriage. Thank You for loving me too much to leave me as I was, stumbling down the wrong road with an ugly heart. Thank you for taking me to a place of brokenness so I could have a teachable spirit that you were able to work with. AND THANK YOU for this ministry who consistently gave me hope while also correcting my behavior and getting my heart right with you. I truly have found the One whom I love. And it's You, Lord.

Dear Hurting Heart,

You're going to make it. You are going to get through this season in your life. God wanted me to tell you that. I want to really encourage you to surrender it all to Him, because He IS the only One who can fix your broken heart. And before He heals your marriage, He wants to heal your heart. Cry out to Him, talk to Him in the darkest moments of this journey, because they will be dark--but these are the moments where you will find you have grown the most. And then the better days come ahead. Take as much as you can for this life-changing time in your life. What seems like its forever now, will turn out to be a short season in your life if you find Him in the process.

I am praying for you and don't forget that Jesus is standing at the right hand of God also praying for you. Take heart in that!

Next Valerie submitted this Praise Report:

I would like to submit a restored marriage praise report (I will send in my testimony, but wasn't sure where to do it!) **Since Valerie mentioned this, we've added the link in many locations, such as on the top of our RMT Page.**

I hadn't talked to my husband in six months and he filed for divorce about two months ago. I did not sign the papers and that made all the difference. God had been knocking on the door of my husband's heart for a couple of months, and it's when I didn't sign the papers that my husband didn't feel he could ignore God anymore.

Our divorce was only 10 days from proceeding to the next step when he called and dropped it. He called two days after I had an absolute breakdown--it was the worst day of my six months because someone tried to set me up with someone else! And it was at that point that I just could not stop crying. It really hurt my heart to see how casually people talked about divorce and remarriage and that my divorce hadn't even gone through!! Already people were trying to set me up with other people. Little did I know, at the point, when I was crying out to the Lord, He was moving in my husband's life!

Ladies, I cannot tell you in words how wonderful the Lord is--how faithful He has been to me throughout this entire journey. Right down to the very last detail of when I moved back home and my husband showed me his new Bible--which happened to be the EXACT same Bible as I was carrying and neither of us knew it.

It's amazing how God remembers EACH and everything. He is the Master of the little details and each time a new one is revealed to me, I can't help but smile. I apologize my praise report is not more detailed, but this just happened two days ago and I moved across country so I'm still trying to process and catch up!

"For I know the plans I have for you," says the Lord. "They are plans for good and not for disaster, to give you a future and a hope. In those days when you pray, I will listen. If you look for me wholeheartedly, you will find me. I will be found by you," says the Lord. "I will end your captivity and restore your fortunes. I will gather you out of the

nations where I sent you and will bring you home again to your own land." (Jeremiah 29:11-14 NLT)

I held on to this verse for dear life. This is an important Scripture to memorize because it continually reminded me that although I had no idea what the future held, I knew Who held the future! We need to KNOW that the Lord has plans for us and they are nothing but good plans for us. The Lord has indeed gathered me from the nation where He sent me and brought me back home!

~ *Valerie in Illinois*

"My Restored Marriage Testimony!"

Valerie, so now tell us how did your restoration actually begin, from the beginning of your relationship?

My husband and I had been best friends since college. We were drawn to each other because of our shared love for the Lord. He was my best friend in college when my father passed away very unexpectedly in an accident. We had been best friends for a few years before the Lord brought us together in an unexpected way. We eventually were married! Then after being married for about a year, my husband got a new job that resulted in us having to move eight hours away from home. It was A LOT of transition as he was constantly on the road and I was alone a lot. However, the real trouble began when my husband became very ill. The doctors couldn't figure out why he was so sick, so they diagnosed him with an anxiety disorder-—something he had never battled before. That's when they put him on an anxiety drug that had many, many negative side effects. One of the biggest side effects is a numbing to consequences and an increase in "risky behavior." My husband actually began indulging in gambling, excessive drinking, and other things. But that man who used to care so deeply about everything, was now so nonchalant about everything.

So, like everyone, we went to counseling. And sadly the counselor prescribed MORE prescriptions. At that point, he became an absolute stranger to me, to his family, and to his friends. In the meantime, I had developed a suspicious, contentious, nagging, grudge-holding attitude.

EVERYONE was so focused on the "sins" my husband was doing, that I came off as being the perfect wife to myself, to my husband, to outsiders. But God knew better. He knew how ugly and hardened my heart had begun to be.

We continued to "fight" for our marriage on our own accord, but I never really sought the Lord about it. I "prayed" but I didn't surrender it to Him. Finally, it all came to a climax as I found out "one more thing" my husband had been doing and I blew up. It was a year with one thing after another with him and I just couldn't do it anymore. I gave him an ultimatum and let's just say, I didn't win. My husband eventually asked me to leave.

Thankfully, there was never another woman or a hate wall between us. It was simply my husband saying he felt he missed out on a lot in his life and that we could find each other, maybe later on in life, again since we were so young when we'd met. It was only by the grace of God I wasn't competing with another woman...nevertheless, I was now competing with the unfollowed dreams, his dreams of a career in athletics.

A month after we separated, my husband quit his high-paying job and left on a basketball tour. I was devastated as I felt the Lord was rewarding him and punishing me. We had no contact at all during our separation. Wisely, I stayed off of social media and ignored communication from ANYONE who I thought would discourage me.

But before I left my home and returned to my parent's house, my husband asked me to find the Lord again and get close to Him. He wrote me a letter that told me to give it all up to Him and that everything would work out how it was supposed to. My real husband was still in there, somewhere.

What he said gave me so much hope! But the closer I got to the Lord, the worse things got, including and especially the day I unexpectedly received divorce papers. Reading the words "your spouse is suing you for dissolution of your marriage" was like a knife to the heart.

Now Valerie, how did God change your situation as you sought Him wholeheartedly?

Oh my goodness...where to start. The words "devastated" and "broken" seem inadequate to describe my emotional state. But when you're down to nothing, you're willing to do anything, and that's where the Lord started with me. I began to pray like never before, I got in my Bible like never before, I turned off any music that wasn't praising Him. I would study His Word for hours every morning. Then I downloaded a spiritual encouragement app on my phone. I would listen to Joyce Meyer on the treadmill. I would do my RMIEW ministry lessons at night. I made Him my life for the first time, ever. I began to fast for the first time ever. In short, I was on fire for the Love of my Life.

The Lord started pushing and pressing and forming my new heart. He humbled me and started crushing the pride out of my heart. He turned my eyes to focus on ***my*** sinful heart as I was ungracious, complaining and prideful. I thought I was a "good Christian" but I lacked so much love for others because I was lacking enough of His love.

As RMI says usually happens, He worked on my other relationships first. I really disliked my job but instead of giving me a new one like I prayed, the Lord allowed me to keep my job and work off-site since I'd moved away. He convicted me about being under my boss' authority and that made all the difference in my attitude at work. And by remaining and changing my heart with the truth, I was given a promotion into a position that I truly enjoyed!

He also restored my relationship with my mom and sister. Even though it has always been good and we are very close, my spiritual pride seeped over into my relationship with them, making them often feel condemned and belittled.

The Lord made me look at people differently. I was broken that I couldn't help but feel compassion for EVERYONE. I would see a homeless child on the television and be brought to tears. It was the Lord chinking away at my hardened heart.

The Lord continued to convict me. He kept revealing to me things about myself that I HATED. It was so painful. I felt like I was playing whack-a-mole with my habits, personality and unbecoming traits. Every time I was beating one down, another popped up! And this is when Satan tried to wear me out by works of the flesh. There was a lot that I tried to combat on my own and I was exhausted. I would be brought to tears because I felt like such a horrible person. But once I got back into the word, I realized how gentle and loving my heavenly Lord is and that these feelings weren't from Him. The closer I got to Him, the more empowered I was through His strength to break off these ugly parts of myself.

As my relationship with Him grew, I finally believed His desire was to heal my marriage. But to everyone else, it looked impossible. My husband was traveling the country and looked to everyone that he was living his dream. I hadn't heard from him AT ALL. The only contact that I had about him was from debt collectors. Then I received divorce papers that my husband filed the day after my birthday. It hurt so much, but I didn't fall apart. The Lord had already warned me that divorce papers would come. In fact, I had been praying against the papers for months and never received any. Then I read one of my lessons that encouraged me to stop resisting divorce and let the Lord's will be done. I finally told the Lord that if it was in His will, that to let the divorce papers come. They literally came a WEEK later! As much as it pained me to see the papers, I couldn't help but thank the Lord that He waited until I was completely surrendered to Him and ready to be taken deeper into the valley.

What principles, from God's Word (or through our resources), did the Lord teach you Valerie during this trial?

I learned to lean on Him for EVERYTHING. From dealing with clients at work, to sharing about my new Love to others, to paying my bills, to healing my marriage, to even turning off certain TV shows that He convicted me about. I learned how ugly my heart was and to get the plank out of my eye and not be concerned about the sliver in the eyes of others.

I actually learned what He said about a lot of things! Things that I didn't really know He had words on. I learned how impossible it was to live a Godly life apart from His word. I learned to let His words sink into my heart so they could pour out from my life and into the lives of others.

I learned to stop complaining, stop judging, stop holding grudges, stop depending on man—this list could go on and on. I'm not saying I've mastered all of these things, far from it. They are just things that I have been convicted about and trust He will change in me.

I also learned specifically from this ministry my role as a wife and the principle of not hiring a lawyer or needing to sign the papers. Ladies, if it comes down to this, please follow the principles. When I finally heard from my husband six months into our separation, it was because he found out I hadn't signed or asked for anything and he said it made him have hope. He said that God spoke to him for a long time, but it wasn't until I didn't sign the papers that God was speaking loudly enough to him for him to reach out to Him.

What were the most difficult times that God helped you through?

I feel like crying thinking of this question. The God that I abandoned (I was still a Christian but clearly not the one I thought I was), had never left me alone. There were some very dark days on this journey, including the week before my husband asked me to leave. He was so mean to me (because I hadn't let him go) and he had never been unkind to me in all my years of knowing him.

The Lord was faithful to me and beside me during times when I had to get my own health insurance, answer the phone to debt collectors, when other people tried to set me up on dates, when I got divorce papers, when I told my family I wouldn't be signing or asking for anything (they supported me but it was hard because I used my dad's life insurance money to buy our home and pay for many things), and the list goes on.

There were nights where I would wake up and be wide awake and the Lord would whisper quietly and loving to me. This usually came in the form of just Scriptures that would pop into my head. I would fall asleep talking to my Heavenly Husband.

My birthday was difficult, Thanksgiving was hard (I actually got a second "official" round of papers during my Thanksgiving dinner with family) and Christmas was VERY hard. And then I had to get through New Year's Eve. Everything in the matter of two months! It was a constant reminder that my family dynamic and holidays were all changing. But there was so much comfort with the Lord as my Husband. I felt whole.

Valerie, what would you say was the "turning point" of your restoration?

If you are reading your lessons daily, you will know that it gets VERY hard right before you are restored. Oh my, how true this is!!

I was asked by a friend to walk in a bridal gown fashion show with her. In this show, we each wore a wedding dress. That was a little difficult, but being around LOTS of wedding planning vendors and having them ask me when my big day was, hurt so much! Not to mention, my hair and makeup artist started asking me about my husband and I told them that I was going through a divorce. She actually tried to high five me! I think that was one of the worst parts for me--how casually people treated this divorce and divorce in general. How it was no big deal and it was almost like a "right of passage." That broke my heart. And on that same day, one of the other ladies I met that was walking in the show tried to set me up with a friend who also just got divorced. I politely declined and then she proceeded to pull up pictures of him and talk about how he was a surgeon, etc. I felt like I was suffocating!!!

After the wedding fair, I started to cry. And while that may seem like an understandable response to being surrounded by lots of happy women planning their wedding and seeing myself in a wedding gown again, that's not the kind of crying that I did. I didn't cry much throughout this journey, at least never in front of others. I cried so hard to a point where I simply could not get a hold of myself.

And then I was with family and friends about an hour later, and I cried so hard before I went into the restaurant with them. I had never been unable to control my emotions throughout this whole journey in front of others. Sure, I would cry alone with the Lord, but I never cried in front of others. But it was like something had broken open inside of me. During dinner, I was in mid-sentence talking with friends when I just burst into tears. We weren't even talking about me or my marriage or husband. I ran into the restaurant bathroom and just sat on the floor and cried and cried and cried. My friends and sister came in and just sat with me while I cried.

I still to this point, am very bewildered at my emotions that day. Of all the things that had happened to me over the past year, and especially the final six months of my journey, this was not a day that warranted tears. It was the most I had cried during the entire journey. When I got home, I continued to cry until I finally fell asleep.

Two days later...my husband called.

So please tell us HOW happened.

After that incredibly difficult Saturday, I woke up Monday morning at 7:30 am to a missed phone call. Missed phone calls always gave me so much dread because it was usually a debt collector or the mortgage company calling me looking for my husband. It was honestly never good news. I saw that the number was from the state where I previously lived. The only number that calls me from that state is my prescription store. I called back and heard "hello" on the other end of the line and I recognized my husband's voice. This was the first time we had talked in months and months.

It was a somewhat scary conversation to have because he didn't tell me *why* he was calling. He just asked me a lot of questions like where I was living, where I worked, if I was seeing anyone and why I hadn't signed the divorce papers. I had to lay it all out there and that was so hard! When he heard that I still had my job from the state where we lived and I'd explained why I didn't sign the papers, that's when my husband told me God had been speaking to him for so long and he finally couldn't ignore His voice anymore. The Lord had brought him pretty low to depression and he was tired of running.

It turns out...that the basketball tour that the Lord allowed him to have, was a Christian tour filled with Christian men and coaches that prayed for our marriage and spoke to my husband about the commitment of marriage--something I prayed to the Lord for. Previously, my husband had been around people that may have led him off track, so I prayed that the Lord would separate him from those people and bring people into his life who would speak truth to him. The Lord is so faithful! My husband did receive an offer to play professional basketball, but he actually turned it down because God told him that if he left our marriage, he was out of His will.

I wish I could write in words all of the other little things that the Lord was so faithful in answering there are just so many!

Did you suspect or could you tell you were close to being restored?

Weirdly, yes. I kept hearing "soon" in my heart, but I really thought that maybe I was just making it up. But I also knew that I had accepted the divorce and had really begun to let go, but the circumstances (what anyone could see) did not indicate one bit that I was about to be restored. As I said, I had not heard from my husband in 5-6 months and the last I heard about him, was that he was traveling the country.

Would you recommend any of our resource in particular that helped you?

How God can and will Restore your Marriage and the "Be Encouraged" eVideos. I bought *A Wise Woman* Workbook and am just going through that now. Also, my marriage ministers were wonderful in responding to my questions, they said, due to how faithfully I was doing my lessons daily.

Do you have favorite Bible verses that you would like to pass on to women reading your Testimonies? Promises that He gave you?

"We can rejoice, too, when we run into problems and trials, for we now that they help us develop endurance. And endurance develops strength of character, and character strengthens our confident hope of salvation. And this hope will not lead to disappointment." Romans 5:3-5

"Abraham never wavered in believing God's promise. In fact, his faith grew stronger and in this, he brought glory to God. He was fully convinced that God is able to do whatever he promises." Romans 4:20-21

"Yet what we suffer now is nothing compared to the glory He will reveal to us later." Romans 8:18

"She believed that God would keep his promise." Hebrews 11:11

"He kept right on going because he kept his eyes on the one who is invisible." Hebrews 11:27

"So be truly glad, there is wonderful joy ahead, even though you have to endure many trials for a little while. these trials will show that your faith is genuine." 1 Peter 1:6-7

"For I know the plans I have for you, declares the Lord They are plans for good and not for disaster, to give you a future and a hope. In those days when you pray, I will listen. If you look for me wholeheartedly, you will find me. I will be found by you, says the Lord." Jeremiah 29:11-13

Would you be interested in helping encourage other women?

Yes, once my husband is back on his feet and our marriage is back where the Lord wants it to be, I would be very interested in helping.

Last question Valerie, what kind of encouragement would you like to leave women with in conclusion?

I want to tell you ladies that I had a very difficult time praying to God and asking Him for something and then believing with all of my heart that He would do it. It's because a few years ago, my dad was in an accident and was in a coma. I prayed SO SO hard that the Lord would spare his life and I truly believed with all of my heart that God would save him. He didn't; my dad died. That was the last time I prayed that hard until this journey.

So in the beginning, I had a difficult time trusting that the Lord was on my side and would answer my prayers. So I want you to know that the Lord IS for you; He longs to be gracious to you, but also understand that His ways are higher than our ways, and we may not understand what He is doing now, but someday we will.

I want you to know that God isn't worried about your marriage: He's not anxious, wondering how He's going to heal your marriage. He is confident. He is at ease. He is in control. The storm is raging and your lifeboat is tossing, but Jesus is asleep. That's how peaceful He is about what's going on in your life right now. Because He knows the beginning and the end and everything in between. His promise is to never leave you, nor bring you to anything you can't get through with His strength.

Through Him, you can do hard things. Those things and situations you think you can't survive, you can. And you will. That marriage you think God can't or won't fix? He can. And He will.

~ Valerie in Illinois

Ministry Note:

We honestly were not surprised how quickly and thoroughly Valerie's marriage was restored due to how faithfully she did each and every lesson, wrote a beautiful thank you note to the partners at the end of each course, and also sponsored others in the process. We saw she didn't just go through the motions, but poured her heart out into each form, journalling her progress and ever increasing relationship with the Lord.

It was soon after she began taking the our Finding the Abundant Life course, after letting go of her church and joining Restoration Fellowship, that we could see larger trials, and her ability to weather them, drawing ever closer to the Lord—that we knew it would happen soon.

We hope you will take inspiration from Valerie's testimony and use it to overcome what's been thrown at you, and if so, you, too, should expect the same results!!

Chapter 29

Jana

"A broken and a contrite heart,
O God, You will not despise."

— Psalm 51:17

"When I Completely Let Go!!"

My restoration all began when my marriage started falling apart! My husband and I were not communicating at all, and I was terrible to hold grudges for a long time—very unforgiving! We hardly spent any time together, and we were like roommates who hated living together.

But under all the unhappiness I loved him, and never realized he was going to leave me! I was blind to the destruction that was happening in our marriage! My husband left me for another woman he met through his business. He told me he was divorcing me and no longer loved me.

I found RMI while surfing the web, but didn't look into the fellowship the first time. It was a friend (through a prayer group) that brought me back to your website and convinced me to join. Erin's tapes kept me so encouraged—I listened to them in the car, at work, at home—all the time! The books were all wonderful too. The workbook and Restore Your Marriage are so important to help reveal changes you may need to make in your marriage and life. These are the best place to start!

I have two ePartners, one from before I was restored and one who is restored. They have both been very encouraging and supportive! They have helped boost me when I was down in certain circumstances, and reminded me to trust in the Lord. Thank the Lord for His direction and your ministry! I couldn't have come this far without your help!!

God began changing me and showing me all the mistakes I had made in my marriage. He showed me how damaging my unforgiveness was, and my hardened heart. He showed me how I never trusted my husband, or loved him and the children like he wanted me to—as Christ loved the church! God taught me how to love unconditionally, without being hurt by everything my husband was doing. He taught me how to see my husband through HIS eyes!

As I pressed into the Lord, seeking Him for answers and turning to Him for love, comfort, and support, I felt peace in my situation. I felt joy even though there was pain all around me! Things would turn around and work out in my favor most of the time, and if they didn't, I would praise God anyway—knowing it was for my good in some way! I found peace in all things, because I was living for Jesus and no longer living for myself or for my husband!!

God taught me to be a loving, peaceful wife. I learned to NOT BE a contentious woman! He showed me how to stop sneaking around looking through my husband's things for proof that he was not being faithful. I started to love my children and lead them to the Lord, learning to depend on Him for all our needs while the Lord led me and comforted me! I began to get out of my husband's way, and he started to lead our family!! I learned to be in agreement with him in all things.

God helped me through the divorce papers, just being able to read them and respond to my husband regarding all of his conditions (in which after learning RMI's principles, I agreed to whatever he wanted). He also helped me through the pain of having my husband move the other woman to our area—which hurt tremendously! I did not want her anywhere near me or my family!! But God had a plan, so I trusted Him, and continue to believe His word.

I believe that finally letting go was our turning point! It took a long time for me to quit calling him because we talked often about the kids, etc. Once I COMPLETELY let go, and handled everything on my own, he seemed to miss me more. He called often, he came over more, and spent more time with us! I believe it wasn't till then that I could see how much he was being drawn to me. That's when he began making many wonderful comments about us!

We were having lunch together when he told me he wanted to come home, but he didn't know how to tell the other woman! We cried and held each other!! He hurt over the pain he caused everyone involved and hurt over the pain he was going to cause the other woman when leaving her. It was another couple of weeks before he actually came home, due to the circumstances. It was actually another three months before he moved his things home.

My restoration was slow and full of trials, but I am very thankful to God for it! God knew it would happen just as He had planned!! I certainly grew more patience during this trial!!

~ *Jana in Arkansas*

"Thank God I found RMI !!"

In March, my husband left me intending to marry his "love." I sought help and prayer from Restore Ministries, and purchased the books and tapes to read and listen to. I was devastated!

However, I read the book and listened to the tapes daily. Then, praise the Lord just a couple of days before divorce was to be final, my husband canceled it! It was only the Lord who could have done this!! With in a few months, my husband returned home in —then, just 15 months later he left again.

As I sought the Lord I was able to get through the days, do my job, and attend to personal items. I did have a couple of accidents because I was so shaky and nervous. I ate sunflower seeds, but thankfully did not resort to more addictive things. I became more submissive minded and developed more patience. I was also able to continue my church music ministry and slept with my Bible (reading it until I fell asleep)—it was such a comfort!

As I sought the Lord, God began to change my situation! My husband began to call me and talk on the phone. I just kept telling him I loved him and gave him to God and I would keep on praying. At the point when "she" wanted just a weekly affair, he said "no" and the relationship was ended! He called me and we began seriously discussing his return!!

God taught me many principles that led to my restoration. I learned to spend more time in God's Word, in prayer, and learned to depend on the Lord for daily sustenance: of body and soul. At one point, I felt the Lord saying, "He'll be back." From that point on, I felt more positive about my restoration! I really became aware of the verses in the Bible about why a husband would want, or not want, his wife. I worked through the workbook about tearing my house down.

It was all so difficult, but God brought me through! My nerves were shattered, my stomach was twisted, and eating was a problem. For the first time in my life, I didn't want food! Supermarkets made me sick!!

When this all began, at the beginning of my restoration journey, I often cried during the church service, with tears running down my cheeks as I directed the choir.

The real turning point of my restoration had to have been when my husband canceled the divorce—and said his faith in prayer was renewed!

When my husband returned, he did not return to church for a time. It took six months, and then at Christmas time he came back to church. Yes, I wanted to shout about it all! The church people were friendly and welcomed his return. PRAISE THE LORD!!

Thank God I found you, RMI, when I was searching for help on line! Your resources helped and I would you recommend the RYM book, all your tapes and especially your workbook to everyone!

In my present situation, I know that not praying together as much, not reading the Bible together had played a big part in our "cooling off." I shall resume the RMI program and know that God can revive my restoration now. It is so important to keep God at the center of our lives, and follow His Word!

~ Eileen in Texas

"God is Sovereign—I Will Rest in Him!!"

Before the Lord directed me to RMI, I felt as if I was in complete darkness. I was afraid, anxious, bitter, angry, and I had a whole bunch of negative emotions. It seemed easier to hear the enemy's voice than the Lord's. My flesh seemed soooooo much stronger than my spirit.

I had heard the Lord talking at times but I didn't know how to put into place the things that He was telling me. It took a counselor telling me that she thought I was so depressed that I should take anti-depressants to finally get my attention! It took a crisis of faith and a deep search for what I really believed.

God helped me to surrender to Him by helping me see how to put some of what He had been telling me (all along) into action. His main words to me had been to walk in humility and to focus on my relationship with Him, not my non-relationship with my husband. He helped me to release my husband to Him. He strengthened me to let go of the contempt and bitterness that I had been nursing and allowing, which poisoned and confused me.

God changed my situation and I began to feel 100% better. I could interact with my husband without lashing out or withdrawing completely. He opened the eyes of my heart to learn more about His character and who I am as His child. Then my husband started to speak more kindly to me and to seek out interaction with me.

The Lord taught me that He is sovereign, and that if I believe that, I need to rest in Him. He taught me that the ways of the world are not His ways at all. He taught me that anything I meditate on that is not of

Him is an idol against Him. That really shook me, because my heart's desire is to glorify and worship Him with my life.

The turning point of the restoration of my marriage was when my husband came over on Good Friday. He said that God had been working in his life. He told me that the Lord told him to ask people to pray for a miracle, so he did. He said that he knew our home was where he was supposed to be, and that he had bought the deception of the enemy, which is what caused him to leave. He said that he knew it would take time. God allowed me to tell my husband that I would give him all the time and grace he would need.

This is how my restoration happened: my husband's very nature toward me and about being in our home changed. He became more physically affectionate, he desired to hear what I had to say to him, and he began to share more with me. Over the course of a couple weeks, he gradually moved himself back into our home. It is glorious and all credit and glory to God!!!!

I found RMI through a dear gentleman from my church who had known about my situation. He was in a similar situation. One day in church he approached me and gave the website telling me that it had really ministered to him.

Your resources helped me to see what it looked like to act out what the Lord had been trying to get across to me. The Restore Your Marriage book was particularly helpful.

~ *Lindsay in Ohio*

Chapter 30

Isabel

"A broken and a contrite heart,
O God, You will not despise."

— Psalm 51:17

"Acts of Kindness"

Dear One day I realized that my husband and I were getting more and more distant, fighting a lot and getting days and days without talking to each other, I started to think about what would be wrong with us. In some moments I thought that due to the fact of being married for almost 20 years, it would be natural such circumstances. But I got quite bothered every time I sought him for reconciliation and he didn't show any interest in this. At that time I hardly knew that my contentiousness had undermined my marriage and led a completely-in-love husband for me not only to never want to see me anymore in his life, but also to seek in other women that I refused to let happen.

When my husband finally opened up about not loving me anymore, and not caring about his ministry in our church, my world fell down, because, although I was contentious and emotionally immature, I ALWAYS loved my husband very much. So, I started to read books about the power of prayer and put in practice the teachings I was learning about seeking the Lord with all my heart. I also began to devour books of Christian writers about marriage, and thank God everything I read was of great help for me to see who I really was.

My husband was using the excuse of working in another state to stay at his parents' house. He used to be home once a month, or less. In this meantime, I sought God in prayer and fasting and convinced my husband to talk to a pastor we knew as a man of God. He agreed, but it was only for the sake of conscience, so to not say that he had given up without trying. Each one of us went to talk to the Pastor alone. And that, my conversation with this pastor, was a turning point for me, because it was the first time I became aware of the prejudiced and contentious person I was, and of the great need of changing in order to allow God to restore my marriage.

From there, I intensified the fasts so that I lost weight, about thirty kilo (66lbs.). My husband noticed my change, as he told me later, but he was still decided to leave home. I clearly realized the power of the enemy as a tie holding him, and I did not know what to do to make the situation progressed.

It was in this context that I found on the internet site of the RMI and the book "*How God Can and Will Restore Your Marriage*". I absolutely devoured the book. The feeling I have today is that Erin knows me and she wrote the book, the encouragements and RRR online courses especially for me—especially the chapters CONTENTIOUS WOMAN, WON WITHOUT WORDS and GENTLE AND QUIET SPIRIT. Soon my husband started to notice my transformation, and as God also bothered him and gave him revelations in dreams, I eagerly rushed him and charged him for a decision but recognize that my biggest fight and my greatest learning is to let God be God.

Reading the book "*How God Can and Will Restore Your Marriage*", the courses (I'm doing course 4), Reading Psalms and Proverbs, reading the Daily Encouragements and the Praise Reports have been essential pieces for my restoration. I've begun all of this only focusing the return of my earthly husband, but I just learned that I already have the BEST of all husbands, Who, to call my attention and making me His bride, allowed all this to happen to me.

Some time ago, my Heavenly Husband took me and my husband to spend school holidays with each other and to visit our relatives in the other state where he was living. Due to work issues, he had rented a house in the neighborhood of some house he was building. As soon as I entered the house he was living, I felt horrible. I sensed another woman presence there. Later I found out everything in the laptop he had there. It was so, so hard and humiliating. But today I understand that God allowed all of this to happen for my husband to confess to me everything and observe my behavior in this meantime. My reaction from this moment on, motivated and impressed him. Afterwards he told me that he had lied to the OW and sent her to her parents' under the excuse of her visiting them. He did this to stay with us in the house.

Despite of having this conversation with me, I soon found out he continued cheating on me. Again he went to work out of our state. Again we went there on vacation. There he had made plans to take us to live there with him. It was already all set: job for both of us, school for our kids. But, as soon as I came back home I saw on Facebook that he had taken the OW again to live with him. When it seemed that all was lost, he was fired.

In this meantime, I confronted him sometimes when I knew the OW was there. Now I see it was a mistake. When one day, God shook me, I stopped to talking to my husband about our relationship and turned my attention to the Lord, decided to do everything He told me to, even if it was to allow the break up with my husband.

From there, all working doors closed for my husband and he had to return home, kind of forced, because only here he got some work to do. It happened almost a year ago, but, because things did not go as I dreamed, with a romantic apology from my husband, him putting back his wedding ring, I did not recognize that God had restored my marriage.

Many times I came to this website to send you my testimony, but as soon as I started to tell the story, I only could focus on my husband's sin, on how I was suffering with all he was putting me through. Then I deleted the text and gave up continuing. Then, I suffered for days just to remind me of the situation. It is a totally different feeling today. Not that I feel good to remember that part of my life, but today I just can see how my Lord has changed me and how much I still need to improve so that He uses me as He wishes in the reconstruction of my home.

My husband hasn't put back his wedding ring yet, and we didn't have that final conversation as I dreamed of, but in a special program for couples in a church he went to sing, there was a lecture about forgiveness, and a moment for husbands to ask their wives for forgiveness. Since I watched almost all the program alone, I didn't dare expect that he would come to me. But, surprisingly, he came upto me, hugged me, kissed me and asked for forgiveness on the microphone. There was no talk, or other words. But I know how much it cost him. Above all, I know he was sincere.

Since he is home, gradually he is approaching me. When I learned that I should not seduce or chase him and let him go away, he's the one who has sought intimacy with me and has come after me. When he returned home he didn't tell anything, simply went out, disappeared all day long, but it has changed. Also, I notice small acts of kindness like buying me feminine products and the brand I like, sleeping embraced to me when before he used to sleep as far from me as he could with his arms crossed, and going out together with our kids. Although these may seem small things, however they are actually great walls that the Lord comes knocking.. I know that in the due time he will say he loves me and will again use his wedding ring. The Lord promised and He is not a Man to lie.

My husband never got to leave our home definitely. So, nobody besides that Pastor, even our kids, knows what was happening to us. I praise my Loved Heavenly Husband for giving me wisdom and strength to keep this secret. I confess that in the beginning I did this for shame. I understand now that was the reason I went through so much was to learn that all that matters is to be with my real Husband, my Beloved, my Heavenly Husband. He's all I want, all I need and all for what I live.

Reading and re-reading the book "*How God Can and Will Restore Your Marriage*" the Daily Encouragements and Devotionals have been essential to my journey. In addition, the courses have also played a very important part in my transformation. Thanks to the love of my Beloved, I am not the same person anymore. So I will always be willing to answer the call of my Lord, my Beloved and help other women who are also going through this journey.

My dearest ones, we have a real and true God. He never fails, but do not forget that, just like Abraham had to wait 25 years to see God's promise fulfilled in his life it was because he needed to be transformed, needed to have faith enough—so it is with us. Do not fight with Him. Surrender and let Him do what it takes to take you to Him. Seek Him with all your heart and stop chasing your earthly husband. You're not able to take care of him. Only God can. You're not able to change either yourself or your husband. So, give your life in the hands of this wonderful God, love and know the BEST Husband a woman can have. He will take care of you, your earthly husband and your children

~ Isabel in Brazil

Chapter 31

Tiffany

"A broken and a contrite heart,
O God, You will not despise."

— Psalm 51:17

"I am Forever a Soldier for Christ!!!"

Let me start from the beginning so that you know what a tremendous miracle my restoration is. My husband and I were married under "extreme" circumstances. We were both in college and I was 7 months pregnant with our first daughter. I had "knowledge" about God but did not "know" Him to be my Lord and Savior. As a result, I followed in the footsteps of all the other women I knew: I was bossy, demanding, manipulative, deceptive and violent. I degraded my husband and questioned his authority and intelligence constantly!

Then, after five short years of marriage, I was surprised that he was ready to leave me. Years earlier, I had suspected that he was planning to escape, and I tried to manipulate him into staying by getting pregnant with our second daughter, but the plan failed. For months, he talked of having a "trial separation" to see if we could work things out without living together, but when I refused to agree with him, he took it to another level. That's when he decided to divorce me. "Agree with your adversary quickly while you are still with him on the way, or he may hand you over to the judge" (Matthew 5:25). He came to my job and served me personally with divorce papers—I was heart-broken. I tried to beg, plead, and negotiate with him to not leave me this way, but God had turned his heart far from me.

I then took matters into my own hand, so as to show him that I would not be defeated—I was very much a feminist at this time. I gave him an ultimatum that if he didn't give up his plans to separate and divorce me, I would leave town. In the end, I packed up our two daughters and moved 300 miles away to seek the comfort of friends and family from this "cruel, evil man." I had only been separated from my husband for three weeks when the Lord began to beckon to me. I was on a marriage ministry chat line, and one of the members gave me the link to RMI. I ordered the "How God Can and Will Restore Your Marriage" book, and was broken the very first night. I quickly obeyed Erin's principles, and was on the road to restoration!

There were many losses and victories as I sought the Lord for restoration. As I began to apply the RMI principles and study the Bible, I began to change inside and out. Before my marriage crumbled, I was overweight and contentious, but as I began to fast and pray, pounds began to drop off and my countenance became more "gentle." Earlier, I did not see my children as the blessings that Psalm 127 say they are; I yelled at them and didn't want to spend time with them. When the Lord began to convict me about "getting my house in order," I began to realize that not only did He want to restore my marriage; He wanted to restore my relationship with my children and my family also!

I became a zealot for the Lord, and I worked with Him as He began to transform me into His image. As I began to fellowship with Him at 4:30 a.m. in the morning, He anointed me with the wisdom and discretion that I so desperately needed to see this battle through to the end.

As I began to radiate for the Lord (and put aside all jealousy, bitterness, and anger toward my husband, and anyone else for that matter), God began to change my situation, and my husband slowly began to come around more. When God was dealing with me on certain issues, He would deliberately keep my husband away to stretch my faith or refine me to His liking—He was testing me to see if I still idolized my marriage.

During this time, I began a love affair with the Lord that was so strong that I was willing to have Him as my Husband forever! I wanted my husband to come home, but I had the love of the Father and I was finally at peace—what more could a woman ask for?! Like in Erin's situation, my husband began to accuse me of being with another man, and like

Erin, I confessed that I was in love with another man and His name was Jesus!

On New Year's Day, my two daughters and I prayed on our faces that God would bring daddy home. Three weeks later, my husband called me and told me that he had lost his job. We talked for several hours as he revealed the last two years of his life to me: the drugs, drinking, women, parties, darkness, and hopelessness. He had a girlfriend at the time, but even she had betrayed him, and he sought comfort with me, “the wife of his youth”! That same night, he moved his clothes home; within a week we were remarried, and within three weeks God blessed us with our third pregnancy!

God taught me during this trial, first and foremost, that I needed to be quiet and seek the Lord in everything. For many years, I was a gossip and slanderer, but praise God, He delivered me—I no longer have the "need" to talk to everybody about my problems—I go to the throne.

My husband never trusted me, as I always told our “family business” to others. Now, I want to be his crown and I edify him to others and sing his praises.

Also, the principle of praying the hedge of protection around your husband DAILY is something every woman must do. I prayed that the OW would lose interest in my husband, and she did. She moved out of my husband's home against my husband's wishes—he had no idea why she would leave, but I did!!

Also, the Lord taught me to put away any trace of a Pharisee spirit. The Lord led me to read the entire book of Matthew while my husband and children (and the OW, I found out later) were in Florida at a family reunion. As I read the book, I began to see how loving and kind Jesus was, even to the harlot and the socially undesirable. The Pharisees, however, questioned everything about Jesus and were hypocrites. I saw then that I was a "white-washed tomb"—I looked down on others who were dirty or in "open" sin.

At the time of this revelation, I was visiting my mother and her live-in boyfriend, and because they were "shacking up," I would not even acknowledge her boyfriend. I then began to see how wrong and judgmental I was. How I was professing to be a Christian, and yet I had a nasty attitude—this was not the witness that Jesus had... He was a "friend of sinners"! I quickly confessed and repented. Then I wrote to the brother that I had in prison (that I was so ashamed of), and apologized for ignoring him. I began to speak to my mother's live-in boyfriend and brought him a Christmas gift—he was so taken aback by my kindness that he began to call me his daughter. Now I am very careful not to think of myself more highly than I ought to and to always walk in love with everyone—especially sinners.

The most difficult time "was believing God" for the healing of my marriage when everyone else thought I was crazy. At one point, my mother even stopped talking to me and my mother-in-law said that it was what "I" wanted and not necessarily what God wanted. I would run to RMI or the Psalms each time and be immediately uplifted. There were times when I wanted to give up, but I had surrendered my life to God, and told Him that I would do it for Him.

Toward the end, I began to profess my faith to these non-believers, telling them that God was going to bring my husband home. I had seen God's hand in my life so many times that I finally believed that He was going to do this for me.

As my restoration drew closer, God began to lead me more and more into quiet time.

The turning point came when I began to truly believe that there was a living God and understand that this was not a battle of flesh and blood but against rulers, authorities, and powers of the dark kingdoms. For so many years, I heard about God and believed in creationism, but did not have any faith to back it up.

God began to build my faith as He answered prayer after prayer. I became so close to the Lord that I could hear Him warn me about situations and people before they happened! Now, when I need to hear from the Lord, I go to my quiet place and He always speaks to my heart. The Holy Spirit became my Comforter, and I now know that I am forever a soldier for Christ. I do get weary and wonder if I will ever "get it right," but I now know that we must all go through levels of purification in order to be the effective witness that God wants us to be.

This is how my restoration happened. My husband did not come home because he felt "led by the Lord." Instead, God allowed him to be reduced to a loaf of bread, which humbled him enough to come home to his wife and children. God is still doing a work in my husband and me. The enemy is still attacking my husband so much so that he doubts if it was the right decision to come home. I must keep quiet and stay close to the Lord as He transforms my husband into the leader, provider, protector, and priest of our homestead. My husband is resisting, much like I did in the beginning, but I know that God will gain the victory in the end.

So often, when you form a true relationship with the Father, and gain this wisdom and discretion that even older women do not have (I am only 29 and am amazed at how foolish and ignorant 50-year old Christian women are when it comes to marriage and family), you can become self-righteous and/or legalistic. God has dealt with me and will continue to deal with me in this area of spiritual arrogance. He cannot use me or anyone else in a state of pride. Right now, my marriage is the thorn that God has placed in my life to keep me running back to Him and to keep me from becoming conceited.

I would recommend RMI resources since they were my rock when I thought my husband would never come home, when he told me he was seriously involved with another woman and would not leave her for me, when everyone turned away from me and I was alone. I watched the tapes over and over and listened to the CDs when I went to bed at night. These books and CDs accompanied me to work, church, road trips, and anywhere else I thought I would have free time. I pore over these materials to this day, because we can never be too grounded and think we "know it all." Let not a man think he stands lest he falls.

I was a part of the Restoration Fellowship, but it did not produce the fruit that it was designed to produce. I was linked with an ePartner. However, we violated the principles early on because instead of encouraging one another and growing closer to the Lord, we both began to gossip about others and uncover our husband's nakedness. Instead of growing closer to the Lord, we began to grow closer to each other—calling each other every day, sometimes 2 or 3 times a day, talking on the phone for hours at a time, and basically looking to each other for healing instead of the Great Physician.

God allowed this for a season, and then He took me into the desert and began to speak to me about my decisions regarding my restoration and why it was not coming to pass. He broke off the relationship with this ePartner and made me solely dependant on Him—praise God!

Approximately six months later, He brought my beloved husband home. Ladies, be warned, if you are contacting your ePartner daily for "prayer" or "encouragement," this is violating RMI principles and could be jeopardizing your restoration—"with many words transgression is unavoidable"!

I prayed for three years for God to give me the testimony of a restored marriage, I even practiced in my car how I would tell others of how God brought my husband home. Now, on the other side of restoration, I am finding life to be much more painful and difficult than I had anticipated. My husband is not "comfortable" in his new surroundings and is longing to "go back to Egypt." I have been given a measure of faith and wisdom greater than any Christian woman I know, and yet I find it hard to contain all that I know with my "one-flesh" mate. And when I do share it with him, he gets scared and confused and turns away from me. I have learned to just shut up about the principles and Scriptures, but when he wants to "talk," I don't know how to "talk" without ultimately referring to my Lord.

My husband now knows that his place in the home is as a provider, but he still doesn't know how to live up to it.

Unfortunately, I wasn't making it much easier for him as I began to propose that I stop working and homeschool, and the man doesn't even have a stable job! I am still a work in progress! I so much want my husband to walk by faith and not by sight, but God has disciplined me severely when I try to play junior Holy Spirit—I then realize that this is HIS testimony and not MINE!

~ *Tiffany in Texas*

Chapter 32

Arminda

"A broken and a contrite heart,
O God, You will not despise."

— Psalm 51:17

"Restoration Needs to Be Secondary"

How did your restoration begin, Arminda?

I had what I thought was the perfect marriage. There were no arguments, no yelling, no nothing. Actually we didn't have time for that. I was too busy working outside the house. Plus the activities at home. You can imagine.

Suddenly I lost my job and felt my whole world had fallen apart with it. I felt all the responsibility of supporting my child (Who had an accident when she was 1 year old and has cerebral palsy as a result) financially and physically with her therapies, never taking into consideration that I had a husband. For some reasons, I couldn't count on him. Then he took advantage to tell me that I should visit my parents (Who live in another state) and so I did. I was supposed to stay there for a few weeks that became months. Just to come back and be surprised when my EH told me that he had met someone else, fallen in love with her and that he was leaving me. There are no words to describe the pain, shame and all kind of hurt feelings I suffered. And as most of you, I followed different advice from well-intended people such as my pastor, my parents, parents in law, etc, etc, etc. That only made things worse. All I wanted was the pain to go away, but nothing seemed to work until I met God in a way that I never had done it before because it's worth to mention that we were Christians, born in christian homes, both of us. My EH was the worshiping leader of our church, and I couldn't believe my eyes when I saw him acting like a complete stranger.

Around two months after my EH left, I have a friend who invited me to his church and gave a prophecy there and then prayed for me and a prophet told me that God was going to take me on a "trip" that I had very much desired. I cried because I was moved because the trip spoke to me. I thought the trip was one I had imagined hypothetically to go to some exotic island, but I never Imagined that He was telling me about my trip being a Restoration Journey. I knew the next day I went to my workplace and got on the computer and type the word "restoration" and instantly a site appeared, and I didn't even know how I got on to find the RMI, but then, of course, I knew this was the trip that the prophet told me about. I cried and cried to see God's answer to my prayers and more than once I started reading the book *How God can and will Restore your Marriage* in Spanish. I think I read it in a couple of days and then later I started to apply the biblical principles that were set out there, and I could see these really working!

Arminda, how did God change your situation as you Sought Him wholeheartedly?

As I read and apply the biblical principles, God began moving in my situation. First, He was changing me and changing the heart of my EH by tearing down the wall of hatred that my EH had towards me and my EH was softening his heart towards our girls (which happened first and then toward me), which was when he started to take care of us financially.

What principles, from God's Word (or through our resources), did the Lord teach you during this trial, Arminda?

They were both principles that I knew. But first I needed to really understand about unconditional love of God towards me and next that we are called to love in the same way that He loves us, and to also forgive the way that He forgives us. Also to cultivate a gentle and quiet spirit, which is highly esteemed before Him. I learned to value my EH and to be grateful for what he had done for me. Since I had not known anything about appreciating a husband, and to value him, and it is with shame admit that I had underestimated what he'd done for us.

Later I also learned my mistakes, believing women should be independent, having a profession and working outside the home to have our own money. Like most women I thought it would mean I could spend on what I wanted and to give to others without having to give an explanation to anyone. And this meant leaving my two girls in the care of others.

I also learned that I'm not one to control my body and that I should not decide how many children I wanted. I trusted an IUD contraceptive device before rediscovering it is God who closes and opens the womb as He wishes, and when we are blessed with a child we should never worry about the obstacles that we think a new baby will bring us in any way, much less in economic concerns, which if given, certainly He will give to us to be able to support a blessing He gave us!

And also to understand the principle that man is the head of women in all aspects, also as the spiritual head, and that by me to keep hoping in God that my EH will soon take his rightful place as spiritual leader of our family, for which I have now given way.

What were the most difficult times that God helped you through, Arminda?

The most difficult moment for me was when my EH came home first and then left only after 15 days, so I went back to questioning what was going on because this happened. His leaving again meant reopening wounds, being rejected again, and again being abandoned. But every time I had already advanced more in my restoration and more importantly with my beloved HH. His grace alone could support me.

Arminda, what was the "turning point" of your restoration?

Like all other women that you tell that indeed comes a point that we have no need for any other person to survive, and we realize that we do not need more than what He's already given you— that all you want and need is to please your HH. And in truth He becomes everything for you, He's the only One who can fill any void that is in your life. It is then when you experience indescribable peace. Peace you get to experience only when you feel the protection of the Almighty on your life and know that no one can touch you if He does not allow it, and when they do, He will provided each and every time that this happens—whatever trial, it always turns out for our good. Is that with HIM we have nothing to lose, because everything is win win with Him. And without a doubt the unspeakable joy that is experienced with having a loved One like Him—with the Lover of our soul. No one will ever be able to love the way He does.

Tell us how it happened Arminda? Did your husband just walk in the front door?

In my case, the confirmation of the news came from enemy's hands. One day early in the morning in my sleep, the doorbell rang and I did not even want to open it. My sister and brother were visiting at our home and thought it was a cousin of my brother who had come to see us, so I asked my brother who opened the door and to my surprise, it was my EH who entered my bedroom and asked me to borrow the car keys to pick up some of his things (I imagined me, because that had happened the previous times it was to collect his belongings from the house where he lived with the OW). I said yes and he went and told me that if I would not take the car that day would it be okay for him to take the car to work, and so he did.

I told my sister that the Lord had done it and she couldn't believe it, My sister still was afraid that I made a mistake, but I did not want to comment, but being wise I left it to my beloved HH. Suddenly I received a message from the OW attacking my faith, but at the same time confirming me that he had left her! My sister, my brother in law and I started to shout of victory and praise the Lord for what He had done. It did not take long to confirm our restoration via the message I got from the OW where she confirmed their separation, of course she launched hateful words to shake my faith, but I knew He was confirming something that my earthly husband had said. This time, his return was gradual. He said he preferred to leave his things at my in-laws, invited us to go out that night, and then asked if he could come home. He asked permission to stay more than one night. He told me that he loved us so much (meaning me and our daughters), that something was stronger than him, and then asked me if I would accept him the way he was now, and I said yes. I told the Lord that He was all I wanted or needed and since then he's been home a full nine months.

Did you suspect or Could you tell You Were Being close to restored Arminda?

In fact it was my EH who asked me to pray for him that God would deliver him from where he was trapped and that God would return to his family. So yes, I sensed it was close.

Arminda, would you recommend any of our resource in particularly that Helped you?

All RMI resources were vital in my journey of restoration and are up to today. *Restore your Marriage, A Wise Woman, Word of Their Testimony,* Devotionals, Encourager, and Be Encouraged eVideos. But thanks to my beloved HH opening doors for me, I was able take the RRR online courses watch the Be Encouraged eVideos with Spanish subtitles.

I also loved the *Question and Answers* book, and to get ready for my husband to return, *workers@home*. Actually all the resources that are available here are so helpful, indeed they are an invaluable aid.

God, may You always bless the life and ministry of Erin, and all those women whose praise reports encouraged me!!!

Do you have favorite Bible verses that you would like to pass on to women reading your Testimony, Arminda? Promises that He gave you?

Psalm 109:27

"That they may know that this is Your hand—

That You, Lord, have done it!"

"It was not with their swords that they took possession of the land. They did not gain victory with their own strength. It was your right hand, your arm, and the light of your presence that did it, because you were pleased with them." Psalm 44:3

My beloved HH gave me this verse because it's the truth that only HE could do this. Too often I began to think that I was doing so much, for all the humiliation that I was going through, for all that I had endured, restoration was my reward, but the truth is that I do not deserve all that God, my Lord, my Savior has given me. It is not for what I have done, but according to the good pleasure of His will. Just as salvation is undeserved, I do not deserve what God has given to me and anything I could have lost is nothing as compared to the eternal bliss of having met the Man that I now know today. My HH.

Would you be interested in helping Encourage other women, Arminda?

Definitely yes!!!

Arminda, hat kind of encouragement would you like to leave Women with in conclusion?

As for me, I'd like to encouraged you and let you know what I held onto, and that was to remind myself whenever a situation that threatened my stability (stability I've found at RMI by finding my HH) that when anything difficult arises, is to know how much God loves you. That HE is the One in control of everything, not man, and when He allows any circumstances that may be contrary to our eyes or is devastating, that HE has a way to turn them into blessing. So when something bad happens to you, like it happened to me, that you can be glad and excited, thinking that something good is going to come out of whatever difficult thing happens— and be aware that difficult things will happen.

Women, I would encourage you and let you know that God will restore your marriages, but the truth is that for it to happen, restoration needs to be secondary, and then it will happen. Today I invite you to bathe in the Love of the Lord, to rejoice in Him and believe that His Word does not lie. Delight also in the Lord and He will give you the desires of your heart. And when you are going through and living a sorrowful or painful life— expect that something amazing is going to happen. Your best days are living day-to-day with our Beloved, the Lover of our souls, because the truth is THIS is what matters most. All glory and honor and the honor to our precious HH for ever and ever!

~ *Arminda in Mexico*

Chapter 33

Randi

"A broken and a contrite heart,
O God, You will not despise."

— Psalm 51:17

"Restored even after MY Adultery!!"

My husband and I had only been married for a year and a half when we separated! I had never been married before (this was his second marriage) so I did not know how to really treat a man with respect and consideration. That is not to say that he was perfect either but he did treat me right from the beginning. I honestly believe, because I treated him so badly and made his life so miserable, that I began to see him back away from me and lose respect for me.

One of our big problems was our level of spirituality. He was very involved in church and made God a priority in his life. I, on the other hand, attended "at times," but could do without the actual church experience. I basically only prayed when I needed something or got into trouble. I treated my husband very badly and always spoke of divorce or separation. Then, one day he came home and left, stating that was what I wanted.

After freaking out for about a week or so, I began to get it together. I moved out and got my own place with our daughter. I got a job and started to support myself. I had nowhere else to turn and began to see that God allowed this to happen for a reason. He would begin to change me and I would begin to feel the humility that I was due!

That's when I found RMI. I give you the credit for leading me in the right direction. I began to understand that God wanted me all to Himself and that only when He had gotten me to a certain point, then things would change for my situation.

During my new walk with the Lord, I learned to trust in Him only. I think I had made a mistake before of looking to my husband to make me happy and blaming him for everything wrong. I learned that God is in control of things, not me. It was SO hard to give up control and just follow blindly! But as I began to do that, my situation started to change! The biggest change came after I fell flat on my face!

I allowed another man to come in and fill me with all the things I was not receiving from my husband. The enemy sent him for sure. He told me everything I had wanted to hear from my husband, and completely played on my emotions and vulnerability—and I allowed it! This was after I had been so involved in the Word!! I began to skip church and not look at your website anymore because of the guilt I felt! Although I was separated, I was still married, and had become an adulterer! I had reached an all time low!

My husband found out about my "adultery" but still loved me anyway and pursued me like he hadn't in the past five months we had been separated. I could not believe how open he became to me again, wanting to spend time with me every day (when before we only saw each other once a week on his terms). He also became intimate with me again, when before he did not want us to be intimate. He wanted us to work on ourselves and then come back together. He had an elaborate plan, but God had another one!

Incredibly, I met with him one day and told him I wanted a divorce. He asked me if there was someone else. When I blatantly lied to him about the adultery, he gave up himself. I received divorce papers days later. I felt so ashamed of myself. I was going to sign the papers. But then something inside me only wanted to be with my husband!

I immediately broke it off with the other man and went to my husband and confessed everything! We tried to get back together a few times in the next couple of months, but he was having trouble with that. He just kept getting to a point where he kept asking me to sign the divorce papers and would not talk with me anymore! I was so sad about it, but I knew God could turn it around.

I continued to lean on Him and pray for my husband. I prayed for the hedge of protection and that he would long for me again. I prayed that he would not be able to relax or be happy because deep down he wanted me but wouldn't admit it to even himself! He even went to a divorce recovery group and took his wedding ring off! I just sat still and waited for God to change things. I knew He was working "behind the scenes" no matter what it looked like. Everyone thought I was crazy because I

kept telling them it would change and they would tell me they didn't believe it! I understood that they must not know my God!

This is how my restoration happened. After not seeing any hope from my husband for over a month, I began to find hope in the little things that I did see, even though to others, they were not a big deal. Then one day at church, they announced a men's retreat the upcoming weekend. I prayed that my husband would attend. They also announced a marriage seminar to take place about a month later! I silently prayed that he would feel some sort of desire to go. (He still attended our church, but went to a later service offered.)

That very day, I was waiting after church while my daughter played on the playground. My husband came over to ask me if I wanted to go to the seminar! I was pleasantly shocked! I agreed and told him I would love to. I knew that he was aware I still wore my ring and considered us married. We began to talk and see each other again! The next weekend, he went to the men's retreat and when we saw each other after that, he told me he wanted us to move back in together again! I was amazed! God worked suddenly to turn things around and we moved back in together a month ago! God is so good!

I found you when I began searching for help for separated people, and came across your website. The stories I saw hit so close to home that I immediately joined your fellowship!

Thank you all so much for giving me the encouragement I needed to go along with God's will for our marriage! I have recommended your ministry to several people who are having trouble in their marriage and even to those that have been divorced for years! My ePartner was great and very encouraging to me. It was nice to know there were people out there in the world praying for me. I also learned to fast and began to see great results from that!

Praise the Lord and thank you Restore Ministries for offering understanding and hope! I will never forget you!

~ *Randi in Mississippi*

"The Glory is God's!!"

"I had always wanted to have a close walk with the Lord and would pray to Him to draw me closer. However, over time, I now see I drifted from the Lord and made my husband and our marriage my idol. At the same time, I was a very contentious and self-righteous wife and person. I thought I had the perfect marriage and perfect husband and patted myself on the back for being smart enough to pick him. I took my husband and our marriage for granted but most of all I had turned my back on my Lord and Savior, my first love.

One day, my husband came to me and told me that he only loved me as a friend and that I was weak and damaged and he wanted a chance to be happy with someone else. I was devastated. I couldn't eat or sleep and began to turn to the Lord. However, I was surrounded by people (many Christians) who told me that I shouldn't put up with my husband, I deserved better, even that my next marriage would be better! I felt overwhelmed and made a HUGE mistake.

I left my husband and went to stay with my family in another state. This pushed my husband into adultery, which he confessed to me once I returned. He said that he and the OW were just friend, but I told him that our marriage was over and then I asked him to leave.

Somehow, the Lord found me in my pit that I had created, and gave me the grace to forgive my husband. I called him and left a message for him saying I forgave him and he returned home. I wish I could say that our marriage was restored at that point, but it was not. It was at this time that searching on the Internet that I found RMI. I remember reading the words that this was not accident—that I had found this ministry as a preordained appointment with God!

Through the ministry, God changed me. The Lord convicted me of all the ways I had betrayed my husband and our marriage and especially my Lord. I have worked, and been tested (and continue to be tested) with putting the Lord first and trusting Him—NOT what I am seeing with my eyes.

The God began to change my situation. There were times, however, that I felt I could not go on. But each time, as I would give it to the Lord, He would find me and be so faithful to pick me up and dust me off.

I still struggle so much, especially now that my husband and I are restored and living together. It seems things have almost become more difficult. But I know the devil is really working hard to keep our restoration from enduring because he knows the Glory is God's!!

God taught me first to be agreeable and not be contentious. Most of all I learned I must put the Lord first. I was so self-righteous in many areas of my life and I am so disgusted by this behavior and what it has cost the Lord's Kingdom by turning others away from, instead of to, the Lord's Word. My most difficult challenge, right now, is to stay focused on "Letting Go" and "Letting God." I want so much for this restoration to be complete that I sometimes forget how far God has taken us and need to remember He is faithful to complete the good works that He started, not me.

I am very interested in being a part of our RMI's restored group. I feel I need the community and support now more than ever so that I may stand strong and give God the Glory. I know that our complete restoration is coming soon and I want to be careful not to let the enemy steal God's victory."

~ *Tina in California*

"Trust and Wait!"

God bless you all and I hope that my praise report will be encouraging to all.

For the last two years, I have kept silent on my praises until now. Although my husband never left our home physically, mentally he was not here. He was in adultery for two and a half years, and he slept at her apartment every night for two years. I was devastated and in shock, but I knew that I had to seek God with all of my heart and all of my soul.

God placed women and your ministry in my path to encourage me and to lift me up. I will not tell you what I endured for the last two years, but only that I had to put my total trust in the Lord.

After submitting to my husband totally, as unto the King of Kings, He finally answered my prayer, and turned my husband's heart to me, and reconciled us both! My husband has been home every night since then.

I am praising Him everyday and continue to ask the Lord to change me, and to heal and restore my marriage completely so that we can both walk in unity spiritually. Our God is an awesome God!

My word to all the ladies is to Trust and Wait!

~ *Provi in New Jersey*

Chapter 34

Leah

"A broken and a contrite heart,
O God, You will not despise."

— Psalm 51:17

"My Best Friend Again"

Leah, how did your restoration actually begin?

My restoration journey began in October of this year. My husband and I had a lot of issues that I don't want to go into detail about, but after a tumultuous 16 years, the pot just boiled over and we separated for 18 months. I had no idea of what to do or where to turn, but 6 months after we separated I found Restore Marriage Ministries on-line and began a beautiful beautiful journey with God. In my questionnaire I stated "I love my husband dearly, we have been together for a total of 18 years. I've recently learns truth about God's design for marriage and I just want to be the woman, wife, and mother God designed me to be with the gifts that He has given me."

Also in the questionnaire, at the bottom it asked "Are you interested in learning how you can help other women who are in marriage crisis?" and I answered, Yes, I sense this is why this crisis happened to me. That's how I came to fill out this form to submit my testimony, I came back because I felt led to apply as to be a Minister in Training with

RMIOU when they asked me to submit a testimony when I said He'd restored my marriage.

How did God change your situation Leah as you sought Him wholeheartedly?

God first changed me and my heart. He showed me myself and the areas of my life and marriage I needed to work on and most importantly I learned how to develop and cultivate a deep relationship with Him. As I began to change, God allowed my husband to see those changes without me even having to open my mouth. I then noticed the changes in my husband and even in our children. My husband and I became best friends again. It was a beautiful thing to see the beauty of God's hand turning our hearts back to Him and to one another.

What principles, from God's Word (or through our resources), did the Lord teach you during this trial Leah?

I learned to completely trust God no matter how my situation looked. It was a matter of me completely taking my hands off of the situation and giving it up in surrender to Him and I had to learn to leave it in His Hands.

Leah, we know there were trials, what would you say were the most difficult times that God helped you through?

The most difficult time that God had to help me through were the moments when our children we heartbroken from them being shuffled back and forth between my husband and I—seeing the looks of disappointment on their faces whenever they had to leave one of us. But God gave me a promise of restoration and I just had to stand in that promise with peace and let Him do it.

What was the "turning point" of your restoration Leah?

Our youngest son started having issues with his stomach a few weeks before Christmas. I would end up having to take him back and forth to the doctors for test while my husband was working. So we ended up just spending a lot of time together as a family under one roof; having dinner as a family together almost daily began to let my husband miss being a family again.**Tell us**

HOW it happened? Did your husband just walk in the front door?

During my son's issues with his stomach and we just began to spend time as a family sleeping under the same roof. My husband just asked me to gather my things from the place that I was renting and bring them over to his apartment that he was renting. It just kind of all fell into place without me having to say or ask anything.

Leah, did you suspect or could you tell you were close to being restored?

I could tell I was close to restoration when my husband no longer resisted being together, all of us being together in a room; together again without feeling the tension. He started to seem at ease being around me.

Would you recommend any of our resource in particular that helped you Leah?

A Wise Woman was what I clinged to. Even now I still go back and re-read and meditate on that book. But I would also recommend *How God can and will Restore your Marriage* along with *A Wise Woman*. I also took online courses and, as I said before, I just recently felt led to apply as to be a Minister in Training with RMIOU.

Leah, do you have favorite Bible verses that you would like to pass on to women reading your Testimonies? Promises that He gave you?

Joel 2:25 New International Version (NIV)

"I will repay you for the years the locusts have eaten—

the great locust and the young locust,

the other locusts and the locust swarm—

my great army that I sent among you."

Would you be interested in helping encourage other women?

Yes I am.

What kind of encouragement would you like to leave women with in conclusion?

Just Trust God and Depend fully upon Him…

~ *Leah in South Carolina*

Chapter 35

Stacy and John

"A broken and a contrite heart,
O God, You will not despise."

— Psalm 51:17

"Win Me Back!"

If you knew my husband you would not believe that he is capable of such a sin, that is why I am writing, if it could happen to me, a person who did not have a bad marriage, it could happen to anyone who falls into sin.

My husband got reconnected with his daughter from a previous girlfriend in high school—old feelings and wanting "things" to be better for his daughter caused him to fall into a trap.

Yes, like so many here have faced, he had an affair (it still hurts to say it). All the books that I began reading stated God knows what we can bare and does not allow anything to happen to us that He will not receive Glory for if we only seek Him. I could not for the life of me figure out what could be HIS plan for my life by letting this happen.

I was so broken and felt as if I would never be happy again. I did not intend to leave because he assured me that it was me he loved and wanted our marriage to be restored. I knew that if I decided to leave our marriage it would not miraculously make everything all better. So

I decided to trust God and praise Him for my situation even when my flesh fought against it and, oh boy, did I fight against it.

As a result, I instantly became connected with the Lord like I had never been before. In the midst of all the pain and trauma, there were some silver linings that the Lord wove in. I realized I'd made my husband out to be my god, when it is the Lord alone who should hold that place. Men are broken vessels, and not meant to be worshiped. God help us! The searing pain of betrayal made me come loose from this unhealthy dependency and turned my heart in a fresh new way to the Living God—to find my Heavenly Husband!!

It was He who taught me forgiveness...I was very active in my church but never was taught any of this until I found this ministry. How would pastors be able to teach and preach for that matter about something that I knew nothing about? But due to coming here, I realized the Lord forgave me in a way that I will never be able to repay and then I forgave my husband in a way that he will never be able to repay either.

Things were so bad that I can remember climbing in my closet because I felt so alone in the big world. I stayed there and cried out to the Lord. I believe that God did an instant healing on my mind that day and led me here the very next day. It was my flesh that fought so against it. If you knew me, you would say the same. I had a great deal of anxiety all of my life until coming here.

I knew I could choose to be unhappy about this matter for the rest of my days and not represent His Love, or I could choose to follow what I learned in the Bible, it says: "Brethren, I count not myself to have apprehended, but this one thing I do, forgetting those things, which are behind, and reaching forth unto those things which are before, I press toward the mark for the prize of the high calling of God in Christ Jesus." This one principle changed my life.

Well, my husband played a big role in my restoration process, isn't that amazing? One day he was able to walk with me while I was in mourning, was deeply hurt, and sadly was still angry. He said he'd sought God and laid the outcome at his feet. That's when God told him to begin to "win" me all over again. He killed me with kindness because shortly before I found this ministry, He found Encouraging Men. Soon we began to pray together for the first time in our marriage.

We give God glory each day for what HE was GOING to do even when I personally did not FEEL it.... Now today, I feel it and since then, close to a year, we've been happily restored. Thank you for all you do RMI.

~ Stacy and John in West Virginia

"Fertility Problems Lead to Restoration!"

I would like to pass along a testimony I was given by my girlfriend that gave me some encouragement as to how God can move and restore a marriage that truly seems impossible to restore.

Her daughter had been divorced by her husband a few years ago because he had wanted children and was not able to have children by his wife. Eventually he divorced his wife and took up with another woman whom he came to find out he could not have children with either.

During this time that they were divorced his wife became involved with someone else and had a child by that person (she had not remarried), so it was clear that the fertility problem was not the wife's fault. Her ex-husband found out that he was the one with the fertility problem and realizing he still loved his wife and that she still loved him. Soon after, they were remarried and he welcomed the child his wife had with another man as his own, and they now have a restored marriage even with all that happening!!!

To God be the Glory!

~ Carol in New York

Chapter 36

Mia

"A broken and a contrite heart,
O God, You will not despise."

— Psalm 51:17

"I Miss Our Time LORD!"

Mia how did your restoration actually begin?

My restoration began as soon as I let it all go. I would say, about a month prior to my husband coming home is when I finally said to myself, I have to start living and not worrying about all the what ifs. So I started leaving the house more often, and I started helping my dear friend that is going through this journey as well. I started concentrating more on the LORD was when my restoration actually began. This is when I saw my husband looking for me more! He began calling and texting me more often. He wanted to see me more often. It's so true what Erin said in her videos, "at the end of your restoration, you really won't want your husband back. Your time with the LORD will never be the same when he comes home." As she said, I now miss that. I spent all my spare time talking to the LORD, learning HIS Word and just listening for HIM before I was restored. And it's probably why I am restored now.

How did God change your situation as you sought Him wholeheartedly Mia?

I had no communication with my husband for about a month. At first I would cry every single night until one night I got a call in the middle of the night from a "private" number. I answered it and it was my husband. He wanted to know how I (and his daughter) were doing. We talked for about an hour. I made the mistake, before I came to your website, to tell him how I felt and I cried to him. Biggest mistake of my restoration journey! I thought this was the turning point of my restoration, but little did I know, it wasn't going to be this easy. God had a plan for me but I, of course, didn't know it at this time.

Mia, what principles, from God's Word (or through our resources), did the Lord teach you during this trial?

The LORD and this ministry taught me to keep quiet (this was the biggest issue with me). I learned how to stop being such a nag. I always wanted to be the leader of our home. I wanted to say what was going to happen, when it was going to happen and how it was going to happen. Another big mistake on my part. So I learned how to give my husband all control of everything. I go to him now to see what he wants me to do. When it comes to my daughter, I also tell her to ask her dad for permission to do or go anywhere. Even though she is 19 years old, she still lives under our roof.

During this journey I also learned that I need to submit to my husband, I never did this. I was such a contentious person. I don't know that person anymore. I think back to what I would do and say and I scare myself sometimes just thinking of all the awful things I would say and do. The LORD has really done HIS work in me. I am so grateful to you all and of course, to our LORD JESUS CHRIST for showing me the real me, the me He wanted to help me be.

What would you say were the most difficult times that God helped you through Mia?

The most difficult times during my journey was probably the holidays: Thanksgiving, Christmas and New Year's. During Thanksgiving, I still had not had any communication with my husband. He left our home in October, 2 days before my daughter's 19th birthday. It was one of the worst days of my life. After 23 years, this was the first few holidays we spent without him. Yet, somehow, some way, the LORD helped me get through these first holidays.

Unfortunately, Christmas was worse. I already had a bit of communication with my husband but we had had an argument on Christmas Eve. When I got home after spending the day at my parent's home with my gifts I had gotten (unopened) and my daughter had left to see a friend so I was home alone. I started crying out to God and asking Him, "Is this really what you want me to do? Trust You for my marriage? I felt it had been enough suffering and I really wanted for HIM to tell me it was going to be over soon.

Well, as I started opening one of my gifts, when GOD spoke to me, it was a picture frame that said, "Faith in God includes Faith in HIS Timing"--WOW--I got so emotional that night sensing He was telling me to trust Him.

Then came New Year's Eve--no communication with my husband whatsoever since Christmas Eve. It was freezing cold outside, very unusual for my part of country, my garage door wouldn't close and my parents were out of town so I had no one to help me. Luckily, my neighbor was just leaving and he came by to fix it for me--THANK YOU LORD, So, New Year's was also very hard for both my daughter and I but He brought us through.

Mia, what would you say was the "turning point" of your restoration?

The turning point in my restoration was, as I said earlier, when I ***finally*** "let go and let GOD" deal with it all--I finally said, "GOD, let this be Your will and not mine"-- so I stopped praying for my restoration entirely and started focusing on the LORD. And, I began to dedicate my entire afternoons to HIM. I would get home from work and just start reading the bible, reading and reading your books, listening to sermons and your videos. This help me stop obsessing over my restoration and I just started living for the LORD.

Tell us HOW it happened Mia? Did your husband just walk in the front door?

In January, he invited me on a date. We had dinner and drinks that night. We had a great time. On Sunday, I went to help his parents move a wall in their garage that they were going to invert into an efficiency apartment. I didn't hear from him until later that night when he text me telling me that he missed me and our daughter. I replied by telling him that our house was his house and that he could come back whenever he wanted. He said that he was afraid of coming home because he was afraid I was going to be the same person I was when he first left. I told him he needed to trust me but to trust IN GOD. He said "we'll see"--he said, Good night and that was the end of that night.

On Monday, he text me again wanting to know what we were going to do after I got off of work (meaning my daughter and I). I told him that we had no plans. Since he tints commercial buildings and automobiles, he had to go measure a store at the outlets and he invited us to go with him and then to have dinner afterwards. So we did.

We had a wonderful time together. When he was dropping us off, my daughter went inside and I stayed in his truck and I told him I had a great time, kissed him on the cheek and he said, "I will be back." Even though the evening was nice, I didn't think he would be back so I started getting ready for bed. I went to my daughter's room, (since my husband left, I was not able to sleep in our room so I would sleep with my daughter in her room). As I lay there, starting to pray to THANKING Him for a wonderful time and all HIS blessings, I heard the truck pull up. He rang the doorbell and he walked in like he had never left. We talked for a while in the living room and then he said, "Let's go to bed" and that my dear ladies, was the beginning of my marriage restoration that the good LORD did for me. I am so blessed beyond words and it is all due to OUR LORD JESUS CHRIST and your teachings. So thank you!

Tell us Mia, did you suspect or could you tell you were close to being restored?

Yes and no. I really thought times before were the turning point to my restoration but they were just blessing from GOD inching us closer together. I had gone through some really hard times right before GOD restored our marriage where I would say to myself, "What else could go wrong", well lots of things did go wrong, let me tell you. But all of those trials and awful things happening to us were for a good reason, for both of us. They were trials GOD set for us to show us that the grass really isn't greener on the other side as we once believed.

Would you recommend any of our resource in particular that helped you?

The book, *How God can and will Restore your Marriage* was my marriage saver! If I had not read this book, I would still be thinking all of this was my husband's fault. I would have not seen all the awful things I had done and said were the cause of my marriage crumbling. Erin's Be Encouraged eVideos were also so helpful. All that she talks about is how it really happens. I love the one where she talks about the stages of restoration. That really was the way it was for me. Thank you Erin for sharing your testimony with us all and thank you for showing us how to be a woman of GOD.

Do you have favorite Bible verses that you would like to pass on to women reading your Testimonies? Promises that He gave you?

Matthew 19:26 (NIV)

"Jesus looked at them and said, "With man this is impossible, but with God all things are possible."

This has always been my favorite verse. This verse says it all--God can do anything He wants. No matter what you see or hear from anyone, even from your husband, don't believe it. God can and will restore your marriage. You just have to have faith and believe that what the LORD says, He will do for you. I did that and look at me now, HE has blessed me with my family back together again. The mighty power of our LORD JESUS CHRIST cannot be defeated by man. BELIEVE and you shall receive.

Would you be interested in helping encourage other women?

Yes, I would.

Mia, what kind of encouragement would you like to leave women with in conclusion to your testimony?

Never give up. God can do the impossible. You just need to let go of all the worries and give it to GOD, focusing on the LORD. Once I did this, this is when I saw everything begin to turn around. Oh, and when I started tithe and Surrendered and Trusted Him with my finances—Immediately I saw the blessing coming. Ladies, please please, please, give what you have to GOD, HE will work for you. If I would have done this at the beginning, I think I would have seen a change sooner but like I said, all the trials, tears and mistakes I made were for a reason. The trials taught me a lot. It taught me that I needed to change before GOD would turn my husband's heart back to me. And I know GOD is not done with me yet. I still have many things I need to work on, but it's in God's hand and His timing. When HE is ready, HE will do it and change me even more. Ladies, trust in HIS timing.

~ *Mía in New Mexico*

Chapter 37

Laurie

"A broken and a contrite heart,
O God, You will not despise."

— Psalm 51:17

"I Confess!"

I guess the best place is back when a woman who told me about a woman's group that met at a Baptist church not far from me. I knew it was the answer to my prayer as I'd been crying to God for help!

Restoration Fellowship had maybe a dozen women at their meeting and as I walked in I immediately noticed each of the women there had a glow on their faces. Though others have told me I am very beautiful, the truth is, for more than a year only I knew that my beauty was only on the outside. Inside I was being tormented. I was carrying such a huge burden that kept me from the joy and peace I had once known. I was carrying the burden of a secret sin that God was prompting me to confess. Confessing to anyone is always difficult, but the fear I had of rejection from those I loved the most had kept me in bondage, and as I felt alone, unable to confess it to anyone, I had been carry my darkest secret knowing I just couldn't tell anyone. Thankfully that was all about to change.

One evening a few days earlier, I'd had a chance meeting and met a woman who had a restored marriage, and when I inquired further, she told me her marriage was restored by reading and applying the principles she found in *How God Can and Will Restore Your Marriage*.

That's when she told me about the fellowship that met on Mondays. So with my sin weighing me down to the point I was about to break, I finally felt this was a safe place to share and confess the details of me committing adultery with someone.

That night in the Fellowship, I honestly have no idea what that night's lesson was about, but hearing the minister share from her heart, and was openly telling us of all her mistakes in her own marriage, to the point she boasted about them (that I didn't know was actually a Bible principle). But what got my attention the most was the glow I'd never seen on anyone before when she spoke of her "Beloved." That's when I knew that when given the opportunity I could open up and confess my sin to her. I knew she'd understand. Once the meeting was over the minister sat down to speak to me, but stood again, leading me to another smaller room when I asked to speak to her privately.

Once inside almost immediately I began to cry uncontrollably. The minister, I could see when I looked up, tried her best not to show any emotion when I began to share the details of what I'd done, because, she told me later she thought, here I was such a beautiful woman, fully dressed in my Mennonite clothing. My head had a white covering because of my deep "religious" beliefs, and she'd wondered how I could have fallen victim to the sin of adultery. That's exactly why I'd beaten myself up about for several months! I had no idea how this could have happened and why I'd cried out to GOD to please help me rid myself of the shame and burden of my sin.

As I began to confess, I couldn't help but tightly grip the neckline of my dress while I also began to pull my dress down to cover my ankles, over and over again as more of my ugly story unfolded. Once I was somewhat composed, I also explained that husband was NOT a believer but he never minded me going to church without him (just as so many other Mennonite husbands aren't bothered by it either, like me many wives go to church alone). I explained that not only did my husband not mind I was going, my EH actually loved that I went to church. And because he's such a good man, he'd told me he believed that my church was the spiritual covering I needed. I was under the protection of my spiritual leader, my pastor, whom I'd known and loved since I was a small child. I explained to the minister that our head covering we wear is a symbol of our devotion to God and represents the covering necessary for us to be protected from evil. So my mother wore it, I wore it and my married daughter also wore it. Yet all of this was a lie, because I'd not just sinned against my husband, but also against God and the church.

Though it's not as difficult to share my testimony now, nothing at all close to when I confessed it the first time with the Fellowship minister, I hope to share openly now just how this could have happened to someone like me. I hope this can help someone else.

I was actually a registered nurse at the local hospital and it was the doctor I worked for whom I'd become involved with. When I asked the fellowship minister, while telling her over and over how I had no idea how this could ever have happened, she explained how this could happen a week later. That week she and another woman in the group, both fasted for wisdom and came back to tell me what she needed to share with me. She said that whenever a woman works under the authority of anyone, and also due to me understanding the benefits of submission and practicing this from a young age, each time the doctor asked me for an instrument during surgery or to do anything in my capacity as his nurse, I'd begun being vulnerable. This later then led to the doctor, slowly but surely, begin asking me or tell me to do things that I was uncomfortable with, but what I submitted to, which ultimately led to the intimacy that resulted in my breaking my marriage vows! But I'm getting ahead of my story.

Once I'd finished pouring out every last detail of my confession, in order to rid myself of the shame, following the Bible's command in James 5:16 to "Confess your faults one to another, and pray one for another, that you may be healed. The effectual fervent prayer of a righteous man accomplishes much" the marriage minister didn't say anything. When she saw I was done, she simply continued to hold my hand, then bowed her head and began praying for me. I was astonished as I listened to her praying almost entirely using scripture, Bible verses I'd known and memorized all my life.

Later, after reading the *How God Can and Will Restore Your Marriage* I realized the prayers she prayed were in several of the RYM chapters, and also were the some of the actual prayers in this book (though I saw she never once opened her eyes and wasn't reading from the book). At the end she stood, hugged me for a very long time until I let her go and then she told me she really didn't know what more she needed to say, but like it said in James 5:16 she would pray for me and for wisdom.

Right before I left she handed me the *How God Can and Will Restore Your Marriage* book (that I hid in my purse, then the next day bought a cover to put over it before I went home so my husband wouldn't see what I was reading). Though most of the book really didn't apply to me at the time, I knew it would, as soon as my husband found out what I'd done. But deep down I hoped that by simply confessing this to this marriage minister it would absolve me from sharing it with anyone every again.

That week, I later learned, the marriage minister began to "seek God in earnest for wisdom and hear Him clearly" she said. The first thing He told her was that I would have to confess her sin to my husband, but thankfully she never told me until we met the following Monday so I had a full week of feeling free from the burden I'd been carrying. But even more importantly, what she said, was she needed to help me know the truth in order to be set free. The following Monday she explained that my husband was my true covering, NOT my church, nor was my covering what I wore on my head. To me the most startling was why. Why I had fallen into adultery. She said it was "because my husband was not in the position to act as my spiritual covering—that meant I actually had NO spiritual covering or protection—and my sin was the proof because I put myself under the authority of others."

By placing myself under my pastor, not my husband (and when I was younger, not my father), I was vulnerable to falling into sin. This explained so much because all my life, I'd find myself unable to resist just about any sin I knew was wrong. That's not an excuse, but it is a reason (one more thing I later learned through so much wisdom she shared with me the difference between an excuse or a reason for something).

Now for the difficult part of my testimony. A part I don't believe was ever shared. The following week when I came to the fellowship meeting, my face was beautiful again due to feeling forgiven. I knew God had forgiven me and I also knew that the marriage minister never thought ill of me either. So I was surprised that during that next Monday's lesson she never looked at me, not once. At the end, just as the week before, she sat down, looked at me so kindly, but this time it was she who asked me to meet with her privately. That's when I knew what God had been convicting me of all week, she was about to confirm.

That's just another part of what the minister shared with me. She began by telling me she'd actually asked another older woman in the fellowship, Melanie, to fast with her for a full week, and together they knew God would give them the wisdom needed. As a Mennonite member, we are actually required to confess first to our pastor of any immorality, then to share it before the entire church, then finally we are excommunicated (or asked to leave) our church. Then, we ask to join again, once the church feels we've done the appropriate penance for our sins. During this time, no church members are allowed to associate with us. As the minister explained though, we are not merely wrestling with "flesh and blood" but this is a real war in our spirits. The Bible tells us that we don't see the battle, because spiritual wickedness is fighting in heavenly places as it says in Ephesians 6:12 KJV, "For we wrestle not against flesh and blood, but against principalities, against powers, against the rulers of the darkness of this world, against spiritual wickedness in high places."

So when she told me I needed to go through the process set down by the church I was a member of, I told her NO and began weeping and begging her not to make me! She of course said it was not her making me, but she sensed God had convicted me this was the right thing. And of course, I confessed, yes He had. But before confessing before my church, she said that the first person I needed to confess to was my husband, my true covering. Again I cried and begged and again she told me it was not her making me do anything, but to simply confirm what she (and Melanie) believe God had already spoken to my heart. Again I confessed He had.

A day later I finally got the courage to confess what I'd done to my husband, and even though he was a good man, he told me to get out, then he told me NO, he was leaving! Then he said he was leaving and he was going to take our four young children with him!! So he told me to go pack their bags. Knowing I deserved what was happening to me, I said nothing but began to pack the children's things. Praise be to the merciful and everlasting God, as I was packing I heard the door close and our car screech out of the driveway. My husband was gone but he'd left our children with me. I immediately called the minister and was weeping from the pain I knew I'd caused my husband, the fear of him returning to get the children— to the point I'd wet myself and began vomiting. I could hear the minister praying for me and very soon I felt an enormous peace wash over me.

Once I recovered, I knew that what was next was confessing before the church. So I called to asked for an appointment to speak to our pastor and met with him the next day. It was not at all difficult to tell him, nothing close to telling my husband, so when my pastor began explaining to me what would happen next, I already was prepared for the process.

The next Sunday I stood before our church and confessed. My pastor told me I shouldn't go into as much detail (as there were children present, which included my own children). Then I had my head covering removed by a church sister and then I walked down the middle of the aisle and out of the church. Normally an excommunicated member would then enter the pastor's office to ask to join the church, but instead I quietly gathered my children and we went home because I knew that was the turning point in my life.

First I knew that I needed my Beloved in my life more than ever because no matter what He would never leave me or forsake me. But more important to me, I simply wanted a glow like all those ladies in the fellowship whenever I spoke of Him to anyone like they did. I also knew that it was my husband who needed to be my spiritual leader (if I was ever given the chance of him returning) . And, I knew too that it didn't matter if he was a believer or not, that God made no distinction and that women who use that excuse opened themselves up for danger.

Knowing I was done living the way I had been, under improper authority, taunted by the "accuser," it was easy to resist returning to the church in the days that followed. Not only did the pastor call and then come by, everyone in the church who knew me did the same thing. Reminding me over and over what I'd always been taught was the truth, that the church was where I belonged but I knew that was not true. Unless my husband brought me to church, or the Lord Himself told me to go (to share the truth with other church members), I needed to remain at home with my children.

Less than three days later my husband called me from a pay phone. He told me he'd forgiven me, and was asking me to come meet him. Immediately I called Melanie to see if she could watch my children, and when I dropped them off, she handed me a bag of clothing and told me to put them on before I met him. What was in the bag was a beautiful white blouse and a pair of red slacks (pants!!). I'd never wore anything but a dress my entire life, but I knew this was part of me letting go, trusting Him and also ridding myself of false religion in order to have a true relationship with my Lord and my lord (like Sarah called her husband). I stopped at a rest stop and put the clothing on (both fit perfectly!), but I still had my head covering on. With just a mile to go, I began removing my headpiece, then I let my hair down. When my husband saw me he was shocked. He stood staring for the longest time, then he began to cry and he embraced me tightly.

After my husband got over the shock of what I was wearing, he wanted me to put my head covering back on, along with my dress, but I said I simply couldn't. Then we sat down so I could explain to him about him being my spiritual covering. We had a lovely lunch and we continued walking through the park for many hours before returning to pick up the children. We went home and packed, as we agreed we should do, then drove a few hours south, staying in a motel close to where he'd found a job right after he'd left me. He said he had planned to leave me for good, but he felt his heart slowly turning. This was amazing to me because that's how Melanie said they'd prayed, for the Lord to turn his heart! And they'd ask me to pray these verses after he'd left.

1 Peter 3:1-9— "In the same way, you wives, be submissive to your own husbands so that even if any of them are disobedient to the word, they may be won without a word by the behavior of their wives, as they observe your chaste and respectful behavior. Your adornment [as a Christian] must not be merely external—braiding the hair, and wearing gold jewelry, or putting on dresses; but let it be the hidden person of the heart, with the imperishable quality of a gentle and quiet spirit, which is precious in the sight of God. For in this way in former times the holy women also, who hoped in God, used to adorn themselves, being submissive to their own husbands; just as Sarah obeyed Abraham, calling him lord, and you have become her children if you do what is right without being frightened by any fear. You husbands in the same way, live with your wives in an understanding way, as with a weaker vessel, since she is a woman; and show her honor as a fellow heir of the grace of life, so that your prayers will not be hindered. To sum up, all of you be harmonious, sympathetic, brotherly, kindhearted, and humble in spirit; not returning evil for evil or insult for insult, but giving a blessing instead; for you were called for the very purpose that you might inherit a blessing." What touched me is that my husband wanted to take me away from everyone, from the Mennonite community who knew of my sin and the shame they continued to pour

on me. Though he never said so, I know too that he wanted to remove me from any temptation and actually called the doctor himself to let him know we'd moved. I was there and he never said anything to the doctor about what he knew, which made me fall in love with my EH in a much deeper way.

>>One day soon after we moved to the new city, my husband and I mentioned a truth I'd learned, after he'd once again told me he'd feel much better if the children and I returned to the church, joining a local one not far from where we where and to put on my head covering. “Christ is the head of every man, and the man is the head of woman, and God is the head of Christ” (1 Corinthians 11:3). Again I told him I was under his authority now and whatever he said I'd do. That day, on his way home from his new job, he spotted a church that said “Bible” in its name and he said that he knew “that the Bible was good,” so he got out and stopped to ask to speak to the pastor. He told him everything that had happened and at the end, the pastor invited my husband to come back on Sunday and to be sure to bring his wife and children. That morning we all sat in the front row of the church. The was actually the first time my husband had ever even been in church!! He'd even gone to funerals, but would only go the a funeral home or the grave site. So having him bring me was beyond anything I could ever have imagined. It was like a dream especially when all of a sudden my husband stood up and went forward for the altar call. That day he got saved, and also joined a men’s group that met weekly!!! That day my husband became my Spiritual leader and also the spiritual leader of our family!!

Before I share more, I need to speak to a few of you who are carrying this burden. I've met many women that I've shared my testimony with, then afterwards, they confess to me that they too have been unfaithful to their husband and go on to say that he doesn't know. May I encourage you dear sister? If you have been intimate with anyone in your marriage, you must confess it to your husband no matter what: no matter how long ago it was or what you believe will happen if you confess. God says this in Proverbs 28:13, "He who conceals his transgressions will not prosper, but he who confesses and forsakes them will find compassion." But there's more. As long as you hold onto your sin, without confessing it to the person whom you sinned against, such as your husband if you were unfaithful to him, you are ***carrying*** the burden of it. And this will rob you of every bit of freedom and joy He died to give you.

May I also share here something else the marriage minister taught me? After reading this, you may become convicted, which is far different than the condemnation you have been feeling since you first committed the sin. The difference between condemnation and conviction is this: Prior to me confessing, I'd been bombarded with all manner of condemnation that I later learned was from the enemy. It felt horrible! I felt hopeless and helpless, which I learned is the first sign this is not from God. The Lord never condemns us, instead He convicts us, which doesn't feel bad at all. It's just a knowing that you need to do something to make it right. And the Bible verses the minister used to prove this is true was, "And Jesus said, 'Neither do I condemn you; go your way. From now on sin no more'" John 8:11. And John 3:17 NIV, "For God did not send his Son into the world to condemn the world, but to save the world through Him." Trust me when I say that though you may go through the fire when you confess (though you may not because I've met more woman who said their experience was not difficult at all and immediately their husbands forgave and embraced them). But should you go through the fire, you will be set free from everything that's ever caused you to fear, all because He is there in the fire.

After Shadrach, Meshach, and Abed-nego were thrown in the fire, in the book of Daniel, chapter 3 it says, "Then Nebuchadnezzar the king [who'd had them thrown in] was astounded and stood up in haste; he responded and said to his high officials, 'Was it not three men we cast bound into the midst of the fire?' They answered and said to the king, 'Certainly, O king.' He answered and said, 'Look! I see **four** men loosed and walking about in the midst of the fire without harm, and the appearance of the **fourth** is like a **son** of the gods!'" (Daniel 3:24). The fourth was the Lord who was there in the fire. It goes on to say in verse 27 "The men were not burned, their hair wasn't scorched, and their clothes didn't even smell like smoke." This means you will come out clean, with no trace of the fire, which is the way I came out of it all. Many women ask if I had it to do over again, would I do anything differently? The only thing I would change is confessing sooner. This would have helped to end the sin that had me bound for longer than I care to remember. The pain, shame and fear of being found out, kept me tied to the doctor far longer than it should have.

So, please dear sister, I encourage you to confess your sin to your husband because everything you fear is what ties you to the sin, and rather than getting better, it will become worse and worse. You will also be vulnerable to different sin, as if your spiritual immune system is gone. Many women told me they deadened their pain and shame with drugs, which opened them up to committing adultery with more men. It's a vicious cycle but it can be broken, He will help if you just take it to Him and use my testimony to overcome the wicked one who has you bound. Your "own iniquities will capture [you], and [you] will be held with the cords of [your] sin" (Proverbs 5:22).

Dear sister, you deserve a fresh start, a new life that's covered by HIS love. Join me in smiling with contentment and joy in your heart.

In His love

~ Laurie in Vermont, RESTORED

Chapter 38

Margie

"A broken and a contrite heart,
O God, You will not despise."

— Psalm 51:17

"He Found Me!!"

My testimony is short but I hope it will help a few woman who are sure that because your husband don't see the changes happening in you, it's why you can't be restored. You are wrong. The first fellowship meeting I attended, there were several women who were sharing the many ways they were handling their wayward husbands. I was holding the book *How God Can and Will Restore Your Marriage* that I was given at the door the first time I came. And I had been applying the principles that I read and reread in the book, but unlike the other women, I had not seen or spoken to my husband in well over a year!! So, finally I raised my hand and told the women that there was no way my marriage could turn around when there was NO WAY for my husband to see the change that God had made in me! I said I wasn't the woman he had left. God had transformed me as I read and applied the principles from the RYM book. I wasn't like any of them!

That's when another woman stood up, she said that her husband had returned home after two years of separation and a divorce (my husband and I were not divorced). And she said to me, "Even though you have no contact and no way to show your husband how you've changed, God sees! You and I know from the book that if we delight ourselves in the Lord, He will give us the desires of our heart! It doesn't matter if he sees the change in you; God sees them, all of them! And when God does move, I believe that it will happen suddenly!"

That woman was so right! God did see and because the Lord was finally first in my life and my heart, within only a matter of 3 weeks, while I was at work, I got a call from a man who started a friendly conversation with me and because I thought it was a client I was also friendly. The man asked how I was, how work was going, and then he said, "You don't know who this is, do you?" When I said, "No," then he suddenly said, "It's me. It's Don" I was about to say "Don who?" - but something stopped me, some One stopped me. Immediately I realized it was my husband!! That's when he asked if he could meet with me. Because I'd started to shake I said something like, "Oh, sorry, someone just came in to my office, can I call you back in about 10-15 minutes?" and quickly hung up before he even had a chance to answer!

Immediately I hurried to my prayer closet with my book. The private restroom in the back of our offices that no one really used, is where I'd begun to go whenever I felt rattled. At that moment I was more than rattled, I was in shock and knew I needed to find my HH waiting for me there. Before I ever had a chance to open my book, I could hear my Husband speaking to me, and He reminded me of all His promises, which He said were about to be fulfilled because I had waited, content with Him only. Only a few minutes later I called my husband back, then he asked me out to dinner that evening if I didn't already have plans. At dinner, after we ordered, he began by saying something I'd never imagined or dreamed he'd say. He said, "I have done everything to get away from you Margie, but I can't stop thinking about you. I want you back. I want our family back. I want to restore our marriage!"

God is so incredible! "Restore" is the exact word that my husband used! Seriously, who uses that word apart from the women (or men) who read the RYM book? This isn't a word that we use often. Most of us say, getting back together or starting over, but not "restore" and it's just one way I'd call this a miracle!

It was the Lord who'd turned my husband's heart and Who had also put a love and yearning me, which my husband said he "could not escape"! So I am writing to say to each of you, you must have faith. Believe! Just like the book says, "...without faith it is impossible to please Him, for he who comes to God must believe that He is, and that He is a rewarder of those who seek Him." Hebrews 11:6. God is able to work exceedingly above and beyond what we could ever hope for, ask for or imagine, once you fall in love with His Son, your true Husband! The Lord found me and He'll find you too. Just cry out to God like I did and have your heart open to accept the Love of His Son.

I'm also here to say, stop worrying if you haven't seen or heard from your husband, no matter how long. Since sharing my testimony I've heard of women whose husband contacted them out of nowhere, husbands who hadn't seen their wives in many years!! Trust the Lord to turn your husband's heart and even to set up a chance meeting, like I heard from other women. Just make sure you are ready! Study A Wise Woman, so few women do, and that's when a husband will leave. I heard many woman warn me of that too. And if you're focusing on your HH there is no doubt He will make it happen once He knows you're all His.

Back to my testimony. That night my husband did almost all of the talking. What a change from the woman he'd left. Though I listened, I was also continually talking and listening to my HH, which has continued since being restored for more than ten years now. The night we went out to dinner, the moment I said yes, I also wanted our marriage "restored" as quickly as he did. My husband came over, got all my stuff (even packing most of it himself, which means God changed him too!) and he moved me in with him. A new place, far from the OW, and later he told me he'd quit his job to get away from her!

Not only was she gone, but a week after he moved me in with him, he began taking me with him on frequent little "trips," each were sort of second, third and fourth honeymoons! This was without a doubt giving me the desires of my heart after I knew I'd completely forgiven the OW. During our separation I'd heard from many people (people I soon distanced myself from) that the OW was taking my husband on business trips with her (she'd been her own boss). It had made me so angry and jealous, but due to the book and spending time falling in love with my HH, those feelings were changed to me actually feeling pity for her. I'd begun to pray for how lonely and needy she had to be to prey on all the men who worked under her (mine was not the first husband she'd gone after). So I knew it was my change of heart, a heart of compassion, while helping other women I'd overhear speaking of things like this with friends. I'd share my testimony, how I'd been a contentious woman who tore my house down, and always had a ready

RYM or WW to give them. God had seen and rewarded every change in me that the Lord had brought about in me due to His love!

One last praise. Another thing I'd taken to the Lord was the issue of unpaid bills. Not more than a week after moving to my husband's home (which everyone said is where "they" were moving together that was all a lie), my husband asked me if I had any bills that needed paying!! In one day he'd paid ALL my past due bills. Most were so overdue that there were fees and he paid for them too, without me saying anything!

~Margie in Utah, RESTORED

Chapter 39

Zandra

"A broken and a contrite heart,
O God, You will not despise."

— Psalm 51:17

"Failed to Refrain"

Hi, my name is Zandra and I'm from Georgia. I had been married for 6 years when I first came here in August.

I always had in my heart that I wanted to marry someday, but, I never knew that I actually would. When I met my husband I knew there was something special about him. I had always been very shy when I dated, but not with him. We began dating and my husband surprised me one day by making a statement saying, "You are going to be my wife." I knew there was something about him, but marriage wasn't what I had in mind and from my expression he knew it too. As we were dating, GOD started dealing with us in regards to intimacy, since we were not married. We started reading a book that "scared us straight" and we quickly married and began going to church.

After 3 years we started having troubles and I became contentious. I constantly started asking him to leave and also began shaming him by my words, which resulted in him becoming distant. I just didn't care anymore! Satan had a field day with me and boy did I suffer because of it! You guessed it! My husband just up and left me. We were separated for 5 years and after 3 ½ years, I wanted a divorce, even though a "still small voice" was telling me not to. But because I was rebellious, I went through with the divorce that my husband never wanted. Afterwards like most of you, I felt empty and lonely, so I began dating a married man (who was at the time separated) thinking it was going to help me to get my husband out of my heart and off my mind. But GUESS WHAT???? It didn't.

I can honestly tell you that I really don't know how I ended up here at RMIEW, but thank God I did. This ministry has brought me such a long way and has showed me so many things I never knew about. It's a wonderful place to be and to grow in the Lord and experience Him, believe me I know!

Now over the years I always told God I wished He would fix my marriage, and wanted to know why I could not get my ex husband out of my heart. This is something I just couldn't understand. I cried for so long and then soon after coming here I ran into him. I found out he was involved with someone else and had been with this woman for 4 and a half years (she was married but separated from her husband).

After seeing him, I realized I wanted my marriage back and then stopped messing with the man I was with. My husband, on the other hand, was still involved with the other woman so it looked pretty hopeless. As I said, I guess I always wanted my marriage and felt that it was hopeless until I ran across this ministry. I quickly read Erin's book *How God Can and Will Restore Your Marriage* and boy did this show me so many things about myself and what I could finally admit, that the marriage mess was my fault. I felt so hurt because of my past actions. But reading the marriage testimonies and all the others made me feel wonderful and hopeful that possibly mine could be restored too.

Soon God began helping me a lot, but I realized I needed someone to be there to guide me. I needed more of the Lord and His love because I knew it would not be easy. Soon after I changed, due to His love and all of His truths, I began to see my ex and talk to him, but knew this was not enough. I wanted to see God move just like he moved in Erin's marriage and everyone else's. When I filled out my questionnaire I ended it with: Please help me.

Thankfully I never went to counseling, so I didn't make mistakes like that. On Friday, December 23, two days before Christmas, was a big turning point for me. It's when I decided I needed to begin helping other woman, and I filled out the Minister in Training Evaluation after I read what it said about IOU so I knew what I would need to learn to help women in crisis.

RMI has meant so much to me. When I applied to become a Minister in Training I wrote to the Team:

My heart is so still so overwhelmed because of things I have learned about myself. This truth has made such a difference in me, because I didn't know I was carrying all this stuff. It's been a challenge but what you all have meant to me, words can't express. You all have helped me to see what God has probably been trying to show me but I couldn't sit still long enough to listen. You showed me it's not all about me and my marriage being restored, but it's more about helping others— thank you so much!

The reason I am interested in becoming a MITC "Minister in Training Candidate" is that even though I never thought of being a minister, I know I can encourage other women very well, even when I can't always encourage myself. There have been many people who tell me that I needed to be a minister, but I thought "No, not me." But I really enjoyed just lifting people up, you know, it made me feel better when I did.

NOW, after being here almost a month, and going through your first course, I now want to be what GOD wants me to be, and if it's being a minister, wow, it will be such a joy to know I could make a difference in one person's life just by sharing what He's done for me and to share His love with them—that's pure joy!

When I read Jesus healed the ten lepers and only one came back, that made me look at myself. I want to be the one who came back and made the difference. I am one who can say "IOU Lord for what you've done for me!"

Now it's time for me to confess with all of this truth, all His love, I still tripped up! My husband continued to come to see me after seeing the changes in me, and we continued to see each other **but against scripture,** we started having sexual relations even though we were divorced. Deep down inside I knew it was wrong, which only led my husband to be confused between me and the other women he'd been with. Then, after us being somewhat restored, he left me again after 3 months after he had promised we would marry. I was devastated!

Surprisingly, this time, once I got with my HH, I was okay, and knew I just needed more time with the LORD. I went through storm after storm, but He was always with me. I confessed my involvement with my FH to the RMIEW leaders, and I was immediately set free from guilt. Then I began to move forward and put all my focus on the Lord—completely letting go of my husband. I kept my mouth quiet, fasted and constantly prayed to be closer to Him. That's all I wanted. That's when He helped me learn to depend on Him and Him alone.

It was at this time that I wanted even more to help other women with marital issues because I didn't want anyone to feel the way I was feeling. I wanted to share the peace I received after I finally put the Lord first in my life and began seeking Him alone; not my husband or my children. I started trusting Him in everything because He wanted so much to be part of every situation in my life (as well as yours).

The turning point came when my ex-husband and I began dating again but that's when I also found out about the OW he was seeing exclusively, that she was still very much in my husband's life. I cried like never before to GOD, pouring my heart out to Him and repenting of when I'd been committing adultery with him (not being married but divorced). I started talking to the LORD and I told Him how I was feeling (not telling anyone else like I'd always done before) and that I wasn't going to start crying out to Him only—and that's when He helped me!

As I said before, He first led me to find Restore Marriage Ministries and that's when I knew it was GOD's will to restore my marriage after I saw the heading "How God Can and Will Restore Your Marriage." Then I ordered the book and discovered God's principles, and I learned how I had violated so many of them, which brought me to my KNEES. I immediately asked God to forgive me and went to all five of my children and confessed my faults instead of my husband's faults as I had done in the past. Then I was led to contact my former husband and apologize for everything. HE said that he had forgiven me a long time ago.

Ladies, God is AWESOME! Even after cheating on my HH with my ex-husband, on March 8, my marriage was fully and wonderfully restored! YES it really was! MINE! I was ***remarried*** on March 8th!! And believe it or not, just before we remarried, my husband began opening up his heart to me and spending time with me—but this time without us being intimate—I just couldn’t believe he wanted to wait too. WOW! God knows how to turn things around!!! Once I told my HH I would refrain, never doing it again, He'd convicted my husband of our sin.

My husband even apologized and confessed that he never wanted to leave me, not ever. I can’t express enough how long I was not ready for all of this and why I asked the Lord if it is His will and He if wanted us to be remarried, then have my husband ask me again—and to my amazement—he did!

Yes, I still have a lot of work to do, but my GOD has got me committed to my HH. Ladies God is AWESOME, the LORD has all the love you need, and He is all we will ever need.

Dear friend, never think the Lord doesn't hear your cries, He does. We can't help fix anything or anyone, not even help ourselves to stop sinning. But God is faithful in every area you need Him in. You see, this is why you are here now because He's heard you cry. Be ready to grow, repent, do the right thing, and know that everyone in this ministry loves and cares for you!!

"Dear Jesus, guide and help this woman and let her know that, there's nothing to impossible for You and You are their new Husband now and trust You only. AMEN"

Be Blessed by signing up to be a Minister in Training so you can focus on others, not yourself like I did.

~ *Zandra in Georgia*

Chapter 40

Leslie

"A broken and a contrite heart,
O God, You will not despise."

— Psalm 51:17

"I Look Different"

When I found RMI I am ashamed to say I filled out my questionnaire saying emphatically I did not want my marriage restored! I know that seems crazy, but at the time I was nothing but angry. I saw the FREE Marriage Evaluation and just thought it was a good place to vent. I thought with all the details of what I'd gone through, the horrible way I'd been treated, like everywhere else and everyone else they'd tell me the same thing, to move on and find someone new. I wanted a divorce so badly, but something kept stopping me. Now I know it was God who was blocking me and finally led me here.

There's no way to count how many times I said I hated my husband and I'd tell anyone who'd listen so many details. Little did I know that once I got to the first few chapters of the course, that I would see who was in the wrong. It was me! I was the contentious woman and none of my marriage issues were my husband's fault. There was no way to please me and I believed a man's entire existence was to please his wife. How wrong I was. I was a Christian and very involved in my former church. It took letting go of my church to finally change fully. Now it's hard to believe that I was openly bashing not only my husband but my parents, everyone, and not one person told me how wrong I was! I'd even said I would never forgive anyone and still no one cared or loved me enough to speak the truth to me. Not until I came here.

The RYM book says that God said, "man plans his way but God directs his steps" (Proverbs 16:9), and that God can change the heart "whichever way He chooses" (Proverbs 21:1). And also if we believe we can "move mountains" (Matthews 17:20) it will happen! The woman who gave me HopeAtLast.com believed these and all the other verses in the Bible. Thank you Michele for believing! I was certainly a mountain of anger, but His Word says that nothing is impossible for Him (Matthew 19:26)! Though my plans were to divorce and find someone new, GOD redirected my steps, turned my heart and moved the mountain of anger I once had toward everyone and everything, sending it to the bottom of the ocean.

By the time I'd found my way here, my divorce papers had already been filed. And believe it or not, while I was still going through the first course, our initial court hearing was scheduled. Even though to those watching, each step I continued taking looked like a defeat, another marriage destroyed, God had His way, and things totally turned around right outside the courtroom. Based only on my attitude change, and how my husband said I looked different, I was beautiful again (he told me later) he suddenly had a change of heart. Walking over to me, he said, "What are we doing here? Let's go home." I said nothing, I just smiled, and together we walked away from the courthouse holding hands.

What happened? How could everything change so rapidly? Only God! A month or so later, after my restoration, I finally finished my courses. I'd thought about stopping because I was restored, but the woman who sent me here said that without finishing and going through Course 3, studying A *Wise Woman*, I'd find myself turning ugly again. I looked so different that many friends and even family didn't recognized me. Everyone told me I looked so beautiful and all that changed was that my anger and hate were gone from my face. If you want to have a complete makeover from the inside out just as it says, pour yourself into the courses that will change your life just as they changed mine. Be sure to begin with *How God Will Restore Your Marriage*, but never stop until you've made it through until the end.

~Leslie in West Virginia, RESTORED

Ministry Note: Since Leslie was restored, we added courses to help train beyond Course 3, in order to help women learn how to minister to other women. Leslie has sent many women to HopeAtLast.com, and many were from her former church. Others came after Leslie found and prayed for them on a variety of prayer websites, which she wrote and told us later anyone can do. We agree.

Chapter 41

Brooke

"A broken and a contrite heart,
O God, You will not despise."

— Psalm 51:17

"He Came Back to Me"

How did your restoration actually begin?

My EH was laid off from his job in the oilfield. We live in an energy state and the layoffs have been awful.

Not knowing what to do but not wanting to go into a dead end job, he sought guidance and came upon a mountaineering school. He has been fascinated with mountain climbing for a few years and this would give him the opportunity to do so and to learn even more and give him a chance at an amazing career as a mountain guide. He also wanted to get out of this place and away from a lot of hurtful people and things. I had encouraged him through the whole thing even when it seemed impossible and despite the fact that it would take him far away from us for possibly a long time. I just felt that it was God's will for him.

My house came crumbling down when my husband started talking to another woman because he said he felt lonely and unloved. He decided our marriage wasn't worth it anymore and chose to seek her attention more. I pleaded and fought for him to allow things to work out again but after finding out he was intimate with her I kicked him out. He got his own place and has gone through some trials with her in just a few short months. He seemed confused and missed me and wanted me, yet he said he still wanted her as well. We got along pretty well through it all when I found your ministry.

God gave me peace and comfort with the whole situation and drew me closer to Him. I have peace in knowing that my HL "Heavenly Love" will always be with me and take care of us while my EH is away. He softened my heart further and filled me with love and joy that I have been able to radiate to my husband and children.

What principles, from God's Word (or through our resources), did the Lord teach you during this trial?

Every principle that has been taught in the How God Can and Will Restore Your Marriage, A Wise Woman, workers@home, and Finding the Abundant Life Course have been helpful through this whole journey. Learning to be a quiet and gentle spirit, patient, peaceful, loving, forgiving. To be a servant. To be obedient and subject to my husband. To seek my HL first and in everything. All of it, He has worked through me to change me and strengthen me.

Though it hurt to hear my EH wasn't feeling loved and felt like we didn't have anything in common, even saying he wanted his freedom to do what he wanted when he wanted without me being upset about it, it helped me find the truth.

What were the most difficult times that God helped you through?

The most difficult was watching my husband be with the OW, losing my job and only income, watching my husband suffer and lose his job and go through difficult trials that I could not help him with, and not knowing what my husband wanted or thought of me.

What was the "turning point" of your restoration?

The turning point was as the time drew closer and closer to my husband leaving for the mountaineering school, he had been having to use all of his unemployment income to buy the expensive equipment. He said he couldn't afford his bills or his rent and there was no purpose in paying for a place he will no longer need so he told me he needed a place to stay for a few weeks. The day he started to stay with us more and more, I noticed he slowly began to bring his things over. Soon he simply began to get closer and closer with me and with us as a family.

Tell us HOW it happened? Did your husband just walk in the front door?

It has been happening slowly, and of course, as you say, it is not completely over since he still has plans to leave for his schooling, which will take him out of the country and away from us for long periods of time. But our restoration has begun, since God has moved him back in with us as a family, if only temporarily, but more importantly because he sees this home as his place to return in between. Since he initially moved back in out of necessity, he sees it more as home and where he will return on his breaks. Though at times he's told us he's here, unless he can find somewhere else he would rather we live, other times he has been talking about where "we" might live when he finishes school and how it will be like we are dating again.

Then last night, on our anniversary, we started talking about what "we are going to do". When he asked what I wanted and hoped for, I did a quick silent prayer and was honest. I told him I wanted to be able to cuddle with him, to love him and to be able to kiss him when he leaves and comes home, to just be his wife again in a new way, but that if he was not ready for that or not wanting that, that it was ok.I truly meant that and had full peace in my heart that whatever happens will be God's will. This morning when he left to go to the gym he stopped to give me a kiss and when he returned he brought the rest of his stuff from his house and told me he will need my truck for the rest of whatever he doesn't sell.

So far, he has not told me "I love you" but has always, through the whole separation, told me occasionally that he still loves me and always will. I would love to be able to tell him that I love him when he goes somewhere or before hanging up the phone, but I am comfortable in the love of my HH and don't need that to be happy or content in our relationship.

Did you suspect or could you tell you were close to being restored?

I had a feeling that my husband was drawing closer, but wasn't sure that it would really happen before he left—giving me more time to learn more and be a better wife to him when he's done with school.

Would you recommend any of our resource in particular that helped you?

I absolutely recommend all the courses. And as I said, the How God Can and Will Restore Your Marriage book, A Wise Woman, workers@home, and Finding the Abundant Life Course, also the Encourager newsletter. All of these resources have been such a tremendous blessing.

Do you have favorite Bible verses that you would like to pass on to women reading your Testimonies? Promises that He gave you?

John 14:27

Peace I leave with you; My peace I give to you; not as the world gives do I give to you. Do not let your heart be troubled, nor let it be fearful.

Romans 8:28

And we know that God causes all things to work together for good to those who love God, to those who are called according to His purpose.

Matthew 19:26

And looking at them Jesus said to them, "With people this is impossible, but with God all things are possible."

Psalm 37:4

Delight yourself in the Lord; And He will give you the desires of your heart.

Isaiah 26:3 NLT

You will keep in perfect peace all who trust in you, all whose thoughts are fixed on you!

Would you be interested in helping encourage other women?

Absolutely!

What kind of encouragement would you like to leave women with in conclusion?

No matter how things seem, keep your heart fixed on the Lord. Do not trust in what you see, hear, and even think. God is working all things for His glory and your good. Trust in Him and He will be faithful. Love

HIM first and foremost and above all and no matter what happens He will give you peace through it all.

This is not the end, only the beginning of my restoration and I'm looking forward and am excited to continue my Restoration Journey to know and experience the Lord even more.

~ Brooke in Montana

Chapter 42

Barbie

"A broken and a contrite heart,
O God, You will not despise."

— Psalm 51:17

"Get Out!"

When I came to Restore Ministries many years ago, I wasn't like anyone I'd read testimonies about in *By the Word of Their Testimony*. I was not broken. I was not abandoned. My situation was different from most who said they'd found *How God Can and Will Restore Your Marriage*, which is why I questioned myself to know why I'd come to a fellowship meeting my friend had invited me to. Everything about my husband made me angry, resentful, and extremely bitter towards him so I really didn't want my marriage with my husband restored at all. Honestly, I just wanted to know how to change my husband. So I had searched everywhere for help, several support groups, paid for help from several marriage counselors (that I'd forced my husband to go to with me to). I'd read so many marriage books on marriage, addiction, codependency, just about everything I could find to help me solve the problems I was having with my husband. He was a horrible alcoholic and soon after we were married also became a drug addict (and I had suspicions was also dealing).

So when I came to the fellowship I honestly had had enough of him and of my marriage! Only a few days before me coming with my friend, I had thrown my husband out of our house just as I had done at least twice before. Then just a few days later he'd come back sorry, said he'd change, would promise to go to rehab again, so I'd let him come home. I had done everything humanly possible. I had followed everyone's advice, what every expert said to do, but nothing changed this ongoing nightmare. Now looking back I'd have to say instead of getting better each time I would tell him to leave, when he'd return each time, things actually got much much worse. Then suddenly everything changed. At the meeting I was given a book that I read and began to learn the principles. The book was *How God Can and Will Restore Your Marriage*. What that book said was different from anything else I had ever heard or read before.

Finally I learned that the reasons for my problems were completely different than what I had been told by everyone. I had been so totally indoctrinated in psychology and most Christian books that pushed unbiblical ideas. I had heard from people (claiming to be Christian) how to make him change, and yet no one had ever told me what was actually in the Bible. Some people quoted verses, but always to prove that tough love was the way to change someone, saying that somehow that was the loving way to act towards people when the Bible really says just the opposite. It was selfishness on my part. Me wanting my husband and my marriage to be what I wanted it to be.

After reading so many "Christian" books, that I later realized were filled with psychology, I knew I could no longer discern the truth of what was right or wrong. How a real marriage was supposed to be. It wasn't until I found the truth in *How God Can and Will Restore Your Marriage* and I have to say at first the words became a sword, cutting through my heart, but thankfully it cut away all the lies. In this one book I learned about the danger of ruling over my husband, like when I had told him so many times to leave his own house! I learned the right way to win a disobedient husband, which is "without a word" not yelling, threatening or belittling him. I learned in the course I took, how to deal with a man who was bound to the sin of alcohol, which means he is not "addicted" to anything, but means he's a slave of sin like it says in Romans 6:16, "Do you not know that when you present yourselves to someone as slaves for obedience, you are ***slaves*** of the one whom you obey, either of sin resulting in death, or of obedience resulting in righteousness?" And this means only the Lord could set him free from the sins he's was bound to. It won't happen through threats or even rehab facilities. And the worst thing I finally learned (but just in time) was that by me forcing us to separate almost always leads to one or both people committing adultery on top of the stuff I was already dealing with!

So instead of helping to fix our marriage, I'd slowly tore my house down by my own hands. It wasn't my husband who was destroying it and it really wasn't the alcohol or the drugs. It wasn't the friends he was hanging out with either. I was tearing my home down and with all my attempts at saving my marriage, I'd only made my life much worse. It actually took me just one week after getting the RYM book, after I had looked up every Bible verse that was listed in the book and marked each one in my own Bible, that I think I really knew and understood the truth. This was the same Bible I always carried, always referred to while the pastor preached, and always pointed to and yelled from when trying to make my husband change! I never realized I was a contentious woman until I'd read the contentious chapter.

The contentious woman was still very much me only a few days after everything sunk in. I realized I could find NO Scriptural basis for the actions I'd taken in telling my husband to get out. So in my very angry state of mind, I called my church and demanded that my pastor tell me that what I had done was really the right thing to do. I'm sure I was actually screaming at my pastor to tell me! I just needed someone to tell me something different than what I was reading in *RYM*. He could give me no good answer. He said a lot and read at least two verses, but not one verse could justify anything that I read to him over the phone from the book. But even without him finding even one verse, he kept telling me I was doing the right thing. That I needed to keep my husband out of our home, for my sake and for my children's welfare too, and not to let him come home this time. That the mistake I'd made was letting him keep coming back.

In all my confusion, pain, and anger, I really was searching for the truth. And the Bible says whatever you seek you will find. Deep down I'd always wanted to know, but I had taken what everyone else said without ever going to the source. Going to God's word myself. After much soul searching, I knew what I'd read in RYM was the truth, so I finally called and asked my husband if he wanted to come back home. I believe me asking him back humbly was such a surprise but once he got back home, this time I'm happy to say, I gave him the respect as the head of the household and spiritual leader even though he hadn't yet changed. That was the turning point.

Let me say too that rebuilding our lives was not easy and it took so much longer than I wanted it to. But each day I could see our lives were becoming much more stable. About two months after my husband came back home he confessed to me that he had been toying with adultery, with a woman he'd met the second time I forced him to leave. Thankfully he'd been too high that it never happened, but I'm sure it would have if God hadn't intervened.

It's been more than nine years that I asked my husband to come back home and I am happy to say that he has been drug and alcohol free for close to eight years! My husband is even a deacon at a church near our new home. Though I am not involved in our church, very often someone from our church will send women over to meet with me. I get to share my testimony with them and they always leave with a *How God Can and Will Restore Your Marriage* that I buy by the **case** because that's just $8 a book that I can sow into and help change lives. And because I also keep the case in my car, I go through all 25 very quickly. If I could say anything, I'd say, don't let your friends destroy their marriages or even strangers that you just "happen" to meet. Care enough to confess the way you were before finding RMI and before reading the RYM book. That's what I always do. Then if they're interested give them a book. Most are, but a few still want to blab on about their husband which is when I hug them and just pray they'll find the book when they're ready to know the truth. I'd also say, be sure to take time to study A *Wise Woman* with your daughters and nieces and even older women you know because it will help you stay changed. Be blessed.

~ *Barbie in New Jersey, RESTORED*

Chapter 43

Sandra

"A broken and a contrite heart,
O God, You will not despise."

— Psalm 51:17

"God Delivered Him"

I first contacted Restore Ministries by sending an email saying I had hit the bottom with my husband's constant drinking and his repeated unfaithfulness to me. I said I had tried everything, every method that I had read for wives of alcoholics, but each time his recovery was only temporary. I was sent the link to fill out an evaluation and my journey finally began to head in the right direction.

My marriage was falling apart due to his drinking. We had become uncomfortable around each other, he became distant and there were never any kind words we said to each other. When I met my husband I really believed that if he really loved me he would just stop drinking. It wasn't until our marriage was restored that my husband told me that he was convinced that I no longer loved him because of the way I was constantly treating and belittling him. He told me that my meanness and pushing and nagging him only made him drink more because he felt things were hopeless. He was sure I didn't love him and that's why he went looking for someone who would love him no matter what he did. Someone he was more compatible with.

The truth is I did love my husband but all the books I'd read told me to withdraw my feelings from him because they were codependent and that I was and had become my EH's enabler. When I came to RMI I was clear in my questionnaire that I had done everything, "tried everything" and I was ready to give up on my husband and marriage once and for all. When I read somewhere on the website, before I filled out the questionnaire, that RMI encourages women to "seek God" I said to myself, I tried that. Because I had gone to our pastor who confronted my husband, so I thought there was nothing more that could be done. After our pastor confronted him it only made things worse and he left the church for good he said.

So when God knew I'd finally reached the end of myself, I cried out to the Him for mercy and that's when, the very next morning, I met a woman. I was getting my nails done and I overheard her telling the nail tech that she had a restored marriage. Just before she walked out she turned to me and said she'd pray for me. When I was done and was walking out, there she was waiting for me! So we walked to her car where she handed me the book that she said I needed. That night I read it through *How God Can and Will Restore Your Marriage* twice. Then I looked up and found the website online and immediately filled out the questionnaire.

My whole attitude changed towards my husband and then just two weeks later (when I thought my husband was at work) I got a phone call from him. He said he was at "our new church" and had been meeting with the elders. He said he told the pastor about his drinking problems. I was shocked since he'd said he'd never be part of a church because of the trouble I had caused before by making his problems known (I used to tell everyone!). It was a friend at work who invited him to a men's breakfast and when he met the pastor, then with the elders of the church, all of them actually told him about Teen Challenge and he agree to go for help. Teen Challenge doesn't focus on helping people get sober. They focus on helping them develop a dependent relationship with the Lord, not on any substance.

So my husband was calling to tell me that two men were going to come with him, drive him home to pick up his things, so to pack a bag for him, because they were driving to next state where there was a Teen Challenge facility. My husband came home three months later a totally new man on fire for the Lord!! A month later we renewed our wedding vows that had always been a dream of mine!

My husband is now the spiritual leader of our family and active in our new church. He helps with their addiction group, mostly just sharing his testimony and urging them to care enough to go to Teen Challenge too. Like me many people think that Teen Challenge is just for teens, not adults and married people, but everyone is welcomed and with the right heart, anyone will change from the program, though that's not the reason I'm sharing my testimony. What I want to say is that as a wife you can try everything, but when you do, I promise, you only make matters worse. Try God ALONE!! Give up all psychology methods, as Erin's says, they're spiritual adultery! Go after God, trust Him and He will change your situation in an instant. Read the *How God Can and Will Restore Your Marriage* that will get you on the right track towards restoration not destroying your marriage.

~ Sandra in California, RESTORED

Chapter 44

Gina

"A broken and a contrite heart,
O God, You will not despise."

— Psalm 51:17

"Give Hope"

Dear friends, I want to share with you that my friend's marriage has been restored!! She and her husband were separated for two years. There was an OM and she was the one who left, as she said her husband suffered with addiction. During their separation I was able to share with her some of the principles that I have learned here in RMIEW and we went over chapters together from the *Wise Woman* book.

What lead to them being restored was their 9-year old daughter was having so many negative behavior issues. My friend had to work a lot of overtime due to having to pay her bills on her own, and her daughter was becoming too much to handle. It came to the point where my friend started spending the night at her husband's house on the days she had their daughter so that she could get her daughter to school easier.

Eventually her husband asked if she wanted to move back in. While she was moving her stuff back in, my friend was becoming fearful that things were not going well and her husband appeared distant. She felt she made a mistake coming back and told me she was moving out. I encouraged her to fast. She had never fasted before so I told her that I would fast with her as well. It's now been two months since that time we fasted together, but today when I went to visit her in their home—

she said something clicked the days she fasted. She said she felt "the peace of God" come over her and she knew that He told her to "fight for her marriage." And then, she said, she's never thought about leaving again!! She said her marriage is truly the best it has ever been!!

While I was at her home visiting today, when her husband got home from work early, I was actually getting ready to leave when he arrived. It was then that my EH called and asked if he could keep our daughter another night; this meant I didn't have to rush home after all. I began to talk with this couple who told me that I am the reason that their marriage is restored. Of course I know it was not "me" who restored their marriage, but GOD who restored it, my HH working through me.

Ladies, it was so encouraging for me to know that all that we do and go through is not in vain. Our lives are walking testimonies to others. As hard as this journey has been for me, I am so grateful that He chose to use me to bring Him glory and help restore a family. I am in awe of Him every single day and even more so now.

Even though I appear to be losing in regards to my own marriage restoration, I am gaining so much more of Him!! And He is Who matters. If the Lord would have restored my marriage when I begged Him to early on in my RJ, where would I be today?? I would not have been sitting with my friend and her husband in their home listening to how God chose to use me!!!!

As I am writing this my friend just sent me a text saying "*Thank you so much for being such an amazing friend to me! I would never be able to repay you for the peace you helped to restore in my life. I love you always, your friend forever.*"

I have such joy ladies!! Again it is not me who did anything. I simply walked in obedience to what He was asking me to do and hope what I've shared will encourage each of you to do the same thing. Pass along the Hope that has been given to you!

"For my thoughts are not your thoughts, neither are your ways my ways," declares the Lord. "As the heavens are higher than the earth,

so are my ways higher than your ways and my thoughts than your thoughts. (Isaiah 55:8-9)

He has it all figured out already. Let's not try and figure it out ourselves. Even if your restoration is taking longer than you want it to, there IS a reason. He's called us to go through this so we can help other women, friends or even strangers, find restoration in not only their marriages but finding the PEACE all of us needs.

~ *Gina in Arizona,* who gave hope that led to her friend who is now ***RESTORED*** *live in Arizona.*

Ministry Note: A month later, after *Gina* submitted the above RESTORED Marriage Testimony on behalf of her friend, we received Gina's very own RESTORED Marriage.

Chapter 45

Barb

"A broken and a contrite heart,
O God, You will not despise."

— Psalm 51:17

"Take My Hand"

Barb how did your restoration actually begin?

I believe my restoration began when God first got my attention. When we married 37 1/2 years ago, we were both in Bible College and in Christian ministry together. Three children are now grown and married. We had been "going through the motions" for appearances for many years. In Januar, my EH told me that he no longer wanted to be married to me. He said we are "good friends", but he had ZERO romantic feelings for me -- I was like his mother or sister. Needless to say, I was devastated and cried myself to sleep many nights, pouring my heart out to the Lord, asking "WHY?" We spent that year separated, although sometimes living on the same property.

I did not understand all of God's wonderful principles then, and wasted the first six months of our estrangement seeking to discover what was wrong with him. I finally came to the point of "letting go", and since God hates divorce I knew that if it happened to me, He would be my only companion for the rest of my life. My EH had said that "nothing" would change how he felt. But "...nothing will be impossible with God." (Luke 1:37 HCSB) is what my HH said.

How did God change your situation as you sought Him wholeheartedly Barb?

In November of that year, God finally led me to the help and support I so desperately craved. I found *How God Can and Will Restore Your Marriage* for my Kindle. I did not immediately purchase it, but while on the way to talk with my prayer partner (who was the ONLY ONE I had ever confided in about my situation), I heard the song 'Restore' on the radio. These lyrics shouted out to me:

"I know you're feeling like it's falling apart and it can't go on anymore

But God is a God who knows how to heal so just give it up to the Lord

And He will restore "

I immediately purchased the Kindle download that day. After just a couple of weeks, I sent my prayer partner this text:

"I'm reading the book now – *How God Can and Will Restore Your Marriage*. It's exactly what I was praying for: Biblically based, not using the world's philosophy or man's logic – just God's Word." You see, God really does lead us when we seek Him alone for direction and discretion.

"You will seek Me and find Me when you search for Me with all your heart." (Jeremiah 29:13 HCSB)

What principles, from God's Word (or through our resources), did the Lord teach you Barb during your trial?

As you can see above, God was showing me the principles in His Word even before I had begun the RRR online courses so freely offered by RMI. I learned so many wonderful principles through the daily study of His Word as laid out in the *How God Can and Will Restore Your Marriage* book. Each chapter took me one step closer to My Beloved.

I was reminded afresh that I am clay in the Potter's hands: "Yet Lord, You are our Father; we are the clay, and You are our potter; we all are the work of Your hands." (Isaiah 64:8 HCSB).

I was reminded that this is a spiritual battle and the battle is the Lord's. "For our battle is not against flesh and blood, but against the rulers, against the authorities, against the world powers of this darkness, against the spiritual forces of evil in the heavens." (Ephesians 6:12 HCSB).God used going to see the powerful movie 'War Room' with my mother-in-law to drive this point home earlier that fall.

I saw 1 Peter 3:1 in a whole new light – "In the same way, you wives, be submissive to your own husbands so that even if any of them are disobedient to the word, they may be won without a word by the behavior of their wives,“ (NASB). I began to put Him to the test. Believe it or not, these words of wisdom were given to me by a dear (now departed) saint at my bridal shower! My mouth is forever getting me in trouble – if not saying the wrong thing – saying things at the wrong time. It was time to actually live by this principle.

The other main eye-opener for me came in Proverbs 21:1 - "The king's heart is like channels of water in the hand of the Lord; He turns it wherever He wishes." (NASB). I finally grasped the principle that He not only could turn my EH's heart back to me, but that He had turned his heart away from me so that I would pursue HIM. I was in the 'Renewing Your Mind' course by that time.

Barb what would you say were the most difficult times that God helped you through?

Since my restoration happened relatively quickly after applying the principles learned in the RRR online courses, the truly difficult times were in the previous year of separation. God was always there providing for my every need. My EH had not abandoned me financially, but I didn't want to ask him for anything, so God became my "go to" Person and I always came out of it smiling.

The time I struggled the most was when I had let go and really thought there was no hope for restoration and my EH put out "feelers" and invited me to spend my winter time off with him, not in the Recreational Vehicle (RV). You must understand, I had not yet read *How God Can and Will Restore Your Marriage* or watched the Be Encouraged eVideos where Erin tells us that when we don't want it, that's when it begins to happen. God helped me through that struggle by leading me to the Biblically-based *How God Can and Will Restore Your Marriage book*. This may seem strange, but I just knew that there were challenges that I would have to face when we were together, that I didn't have to deal with while alone. I felt selfish, and then guilty for feeling selfish. I guess you would say I was double-minded.

What was the "turning point" of your restoration Barb?

The turning point in my restoration came when I began taking the RRR online courses and journaling every day in the 'What I Learned' forms. I've never enjoyed writing assignments very much, but when I thought of it as just talking to My Beloved, it actually became a pleasure. I only wish that I had journaled throughout my entire life in that way.

The next turning point came when I finally confessed my sins that contributed to the estrangement with my EH. I put this off for a long time – writing and rewriting what I would say. He just said, "Wow! Is that all?" and I smiled and left the house.

Tell us HOW it happened Barb? Did your husband just walk in the front door?

When my EH came up north for a family gathering (among other things) he actually stayed in the house with me. And then, in the middle of the night, he reached out to touch me and hold my hand. This has not happened for years!

Then he asked me not to make plane reservations before I came down south again, so that he could come and tow my car down for me. I said, "And when would you like me to do that?" He said, "Anytime you're ready to leave your position." You see, up until this point, he had asked me not to resign my position. Suprising me to, just before the kids all arrived at our house, he put his wedding band back on! The children actually noticed before I did. They also noticed him talking in terms of "we" and "our", not "mine" and "hers".

Barb, looking back did you suspect or could you tell you were close to being restored?

I did suspect that we were getting closer to restoration. When I left to come back north, he hugged and kissed me goodbye at the airport, and a beautiful bulb garden in bloom was delivered as soon as I arrived home. I started to panic a little, because I felt that I still had so much more that needed to change in my life. Erin (through her Be Encouraged eVideos) also warned me to "get my house in order". So I did! I de-cluttered and cleaned and busied myself like never before in my life. Then, just three days later, as I was completing Day 27 "Sowing and Reaping" and sending encouragement to others, my EH contacted me (via text) and gave me the first real hope of our restoration that I'd had in over a year. Praise You Lord!

Barb would you recommend any of our resources in particular that helped you?

I would highly recommend the *How God Can and Will Restore Your Marriage* book to be read, re-read, highlighted, basically wear it out. Also the RRR online courses and Be Encouraged eVideos, the Daily Encourager, including both Daily Devotionals.

Do you have favorite Bible verses that you would like to pass on to women reading your Testimonies? Promises that He gave you Barb?

I have already quoted some of the most meaningful Bible verses in my testimony. I have over 200 index cards chock full of verses, but I will seek to "limit" my space today. These are quoted from the Holman Christian Standard Bible (HCSB) unless otherwise notated.

Isaiah 40:31 -but those who trust in the Lord will renew their strength; they will soar on wings like eagles; they will run and not grow weary; they will walk and not faint.

Isaiah 51:7 - Listen to Me, you who know righteousness, the people in whose heart is My instruction: do not fear disgrace by men, and do not be shattered by their taunts.

Proverbs 3:5-8 - Trust in the Lord with all your heart, and do not rely on your own understanding; think about Him in all your ways, and He will guide you on the right paths. Don't consider yourself to be wise; fear the Lord and turn away from evil. This will be healing for your body and strengthening for your bones.

Psalm 20:4 - May He give you what your heart desires and fulfill your whole purpose.

John 13:7 - Jesus answered him, "What I'm doing you don't understand now, but afterward you will know."

Proverbs 21:30-31 – No wisdom, no understanding and no counsel will prevail against the LORD. A horse is prepared for the day of battle, but victory comes from the LORD!

Isaiah 30:18 (NASB) – Therefore, the Lord longs to be gracious to you, And therefore He waits on high to have compassion on you. For the Lord is a God of justice; How blessed are all those who long for Him.

The Message (MSG) – But God's not finished. He's waiting around to be gracious to you. He's gathering strength to show mercy to you. God takes the time to do everything right—everything. Those who wait around for him are the lucky ones.

And so many more...

Would you be interested in helping encourage other women Barb?

Yes, I have prayed that God would use this season of my life to encourage other women.

Either way, what kind of encouragement would you like to leave women with in conclusion?

My primary word of encouragement to all women is from the words of James 1, "Consider is great joy, my [sisters], whenever you experience various trials, knowing that the testing of your faith produces endurance. But endurance must do its complete work, so that you may be mature and complete, lacking nothing. (James 1:2-4 HCSB).

Dear friend, don't become weary, but wait on the Lord. He is able to do the impossible, as long as you are willing to let Him.

~ *Barb in Indiana*

Chapter 46

Judith

"A broken and a contrite heart,
O God, You will not despise."

— Psalm 51:17

"Asked to Hold Hands in Church"

How did your restoration actually begin Judith?

At one point I was so depressed, I sought help for myself. I was crying all the time. My husband did not physically leave me, but I felt his heart had left me. The one thing that someone impressed on me was to work on my relationship with the LORD and let God deal with my husband. I was so broken. I decided that I would seek God with all my heart. I was so bitter and angry at my husband. I started reading my Bible every day. I read the whole Bible several times using different translations. God was slowly peeling away the things in my life that had not been pleasing to Him.

How did God change your situation Judith as you sought Him wholeheartedly?

I started to share with other women what God was teaching me. There was so much to share with them that I wasn't quite sure how to go about it. Our marriage was slowly being restored, but we still had a way to go. In looking on the internet to help my friends, I stumbled on this website. I decided to read the information to help my friends and to see if there was more I could do for my own marriage. Reading the RRR online courses confirmed what I had been learning in my own Bible reading, which gave me encouragement along with The Praise Reports. As I applied the Biblical principles, I could see my husband's heart softening, turning towards me. He started to show kindness and do things for me that he had never done in the past. We were talking to each other as friends again.

What principles, from God's Word (or through our resources), did the Lord teach you Judith during this trial?

The *How God Can and Will Restore Your Marriage* book gave me insight along with the Be Encouraged eVideos on how to avoid doing the wrong things while working on restoring my marriage. The WORD showed me my part in the destruction of my marriage. I realized that I was a contentious woman. The Lord had been dealing with me in many different areas and changing me. I told my daughter I was wrong in sharing things with her about her dad when I had been upset. I also learned to not share with others, but to take it to the LORD. This makes it easier for the spouse to repent, knowing a lot of people don't know what he did.

I kept focusing on drawing closer to God. I did not focus on my husband or my circumstances. I showed kindness to my husband as unto the the LORD. I kept my mouth shut; I no longer talked to others about my husband. I continued to meditate on the WORD. I had to forgive my husband. I used the WORD of God to pray. I renewed my mind with Scripture to fight against the lies of the devil. I reached out to help others. I humbled myself before the LORD and my husband. I submitted to my husband. I was doing many of these things before finding RMIEW which proved this is all Him.

Judith what were the most difficult times that God helped you through?

God helped me when I felt totally alone. My husband was living to please himself. He was never unfaithful nor did he ever leave me. We were each living our own lives. We did not agree on many issues. Because of things done and hurtful words said, we had a hate wall between us. During this time I felt afraid and very insecure because of the decisions he was making, which did not turn out good and had painful consequences.

What was the "turning point" of your restoration Judith?

The turning point for our restoration came when I wanted God more than my husband. God is my refuge and my shield. He meets my needs. I know I am safe with God as my husband. He will care for me and meet my needs in ways that no human husband can. I no longer feel lonely. I feel so much love, comfort, and joy. I look forward to spending time with my new HH each day.

Tell us HOW it happened Judith? Did your husband just walk in the front door?

My husband started to change in his attitude towards me. He started to do thoughtful things for me. In church he wanted to hold hands. He became more affectionate. We started to talk more to each other as friends. He started doing things around the house that he had never done. He considered what I thought about issues.

Did you suspect or could you tell you were close to being restored?

Before I came to this website, I could tell our restoration was coming by the changes I was seeing in his attitude.

Would you recommend any of our resources in particular that helped you?

I really enjoyed reading the *How God Can and Will Restore Your Marriage* book and watching the Be Encouraged eVideos.

Do you have favorite Bible verses that you would like to pass on to women reading your Testimonies? Promises that He gave you?

2 Chronicles 7:14 (NIV)

If my people, who are called by my name will humble themselves and pray and seek my face and turn from their wicked ways, then I will hear from heaven, and I will forgive their sin and will heal their land.

Psalm 9:10 (NIV)

Those who know your name trust in you, for you, Lord, have never forsaken those who seek you.

Psalm 118:8 (NIV)

It is better to take refuge in the Lord than to trust in humans.

Would you be interested in helping encourage other women?

Yes.

Either way, what kind of encouragement would you like to leave women with in conclusion?

Dear friend, God is able to do the impossible. He can change hearts. When we do things God's way, we can expect blessings to follow. Seek God with all your heart, mind, and soul and you will find Him. His WORD is true and can be trusted. He can restore your marriage.

~ Judith in Indiana

"Willing to Give Up"

Today I am thanking God for a restored marriage. My husband never was unfaithful nor has he ever left home. For the past thirteen years I have felt separated from my husband even though we have been living together. We both did our own things. We had many differences in how we viewed things in our marriage. Because of the decisions my husband made, I suffered many hurts. I would beg him not to do certain things that I felt would end up hurting us. I would try to control him, nag him, become angry, and then feel bitter when I had to feel the consequences of his decisions. This put a strong hate wall between us. I was a contentious woman and my behavior pushed him to do things, just to prove to me that I wasn't going to control him. I did not feel his love nor did I feel that he cared about what I thought.

Because of my anger, being contentious, and my bitterness, it hurt my relationship with the LORD. At one point I was so depressed, I sought help for myself. I was crying all the time. The one thing that they impressed on me was to work on my relationship with the LORD and let God deal with my husband. I was so broken; I decided that I would allow God to change me and trust God to deal with my husband. I started reading my Bible every day. I read the whole Bible several times using different translations. God has been slowly peeling away the things that have not been pleasing to Him. Many things being taught at this website, I was learning from the time I spent with the LORD prior to coming here. I started to share with other women what God was teaching me. There was so much to share with them, that I wasn't quite sure how to do it.

Our marriage was slowly being restored, but I still had a way to go. In looking on the internet to help my friends, I stumbled on this website. I decided to read the information to help others and to see if there was more I could do for my own marriage. Seeing things confirmed what I have been learning in my own Bible reading, and I was able to apply them more in my life. The encouragement from testimonies helped me to see ways to flesh out what I already knew. Watching how other women applied these principles. The RYM book has really helped me along with the videos. I just started the second course a week ago. I had to come to the place where I was willing to die to my ways and trust God's WORD. I had to be willing to lose my life, in order to save it. I could no longer control my husband. Following Christ means that we are willing to give our lives up for Him. This is total surrender and an act of worship to the LORD. Renewing our minds in the WORD and living for His purpose in our marriages.

I can now praise the LORD for restoring my marriage. My husband and I feel very close. I am learning to submit to him and trust God to guide him. I take my concerns to the LORD. The LORD is changing my EH. He is doing things for me; he would never have done in the past. His heart has softened and he is considering what I think before making decisions for us. He tells me that he loves me, we hold hands in church, and we both feel peace in our home. We are both caring for one another in ways to show our love. This has been the work of God. Please apply God's WORD to your marriage and see what God will do to restore your marriage.

"For whoever wants to save their life will lose it, but whoever loses their life for me will find it." (Matthew 16:25)

"Therefore, I urge you, brothers and sisters, in view of God's mercy, to offer your bodies as a living sacrifice, holy and pleasing to God—this is your true and proper worship. Do not conform to the pattern of this world, but be transformed by the renewing of your mind. Then you will be able to test and approve what God's will is—his good, pleasing and perfect will." (Romans 12:1-2 NIV)

"Home is Peaceful"

I want to praise the LORD for what he has been doing in our home. Our home is peaceful and my EH and I are friends again. The hate wall is gone. We are caring for one another. My husband's attitude has changed for the good. We are attending church together. We enjoy being with each other. We both love the Lord and want to serve Him. God continues to give me a hunger and thirst for His Word. I love spending time in the Word and listening to what He wants to teach me. God has been meeting our needs in so many ways. My husband has found work, he is doing better physically, my faith is getting stronger, my fears are decreasing the more I trust in God and stay in His Word. God is renewing my mind with the Word, so I can speak the Word back to the thoughts that come from the enemy who tries to steal, discourage and destroy my walk with the LORD.

"The quiet words of the wise are more to be heeded than the shouts of a ruler of fools."

It is so important to keep our mouths shut and allow God to witness through us by our behavior.

"Wisdom is better than weapons of war, but one sinner destroys much good." Ecclesiastes 9:17-18 (NIV)

We need to be reading the Word and asking God to give us understanding, so we can apply His wisdom to our situation. God's wisdom is better than any weapons of war that the world uses. When we follow the world's way we destroy our chances of being restored or reconciling with anyone. It's impossible with man, but possible with God.

"Jesus looked at them and said, "With man this is impossible, but with God all things are possible." Matthew 19:26 (NIV)

"My HH is Always Faithful"

"In addition to all this, take up the shield of faith, with which you can extinguish all the flaming arrows of the evil one." (Ephesians 6:16 NIV)

I praise my HH for always being faithful. My EH just recently got a new job. He was under the impression that he would be working forty hours a week. As it turns out, his hours are not guaranteed each week. Yesterday his boss told my husband that she had fifteen people to give work to and could only use two of the fifteen for the work that was available. We really needed the money. By faith I had donated some money to help another woman get some of the materials I was able to get free by another woman donating to me. I remembered Ephesians 6:16 (NIV) "In addition to all this, take up the shield of faith, with which you can extinguish all the flaming arrows of the evil one."

Satan was putting thoughts in my head trying to discourage me that God could not provide for us. I remembered another verse, Psalm 118:8 "It is better to take refuge in the LORD than to trust man." I had remembered how David in the Psalms would share a need and cry out to the LORD for help. He would be very down and discouraged. Then he would start remembering how God provided for him in the past. Then he would praise God for His goodness. This is what I did, I remembered how that in soon to be forty eight years of marriage our bills were always paid on time and He always provided, even in very difficult times when it seemed impossible. So I bowed my head and prayed and told the LORD that my EH was just told that there was no work for him tomorrow by his boss. I quoted Psalm 118:8 and told God I would trust Him and not man. Five minutes later he got a call, they found work for him. This was at 8:30 pm. Well, today he worked ten and a half hours.

"It is better to take refuge in the LORD than to trust in man." (Psalm 118:8 NIV)

Ministry Note: We emailed Judith to remind her some of the principles for a RESTORED marriage, which we give to each woman who submits a RESTORED Marriage Testimony.

Remember, just as relationships in crisis get our attention as women, finances are what often get a man's attention. This means, be ready for when financial issues hit home. AND then be sure you step back, allowing the full effect to rest on you EH where He wants it to be. Take a look at a man's shoulders and at ours as women (even women who work out excessively could never compare to a man who works out).

Use your EH as a reminder to NOT make the mistake of lifting the burden placed on your husband by GOD. If we do, the weight will crush us, cause us to lose our gentleness (which is far more important to an EH) and use the time to remain closer to your HH, sitting close to Him watching what GOD plans to do.

Chapter 47

Jan

"A broken and a contrite heart,
O God, You will not despise."

— Psalm 51:17

"I've Done EVERYTHING Wrong!"

When I found your ministry I was horribly distressed over the separation from my husband. Crying out to God to show me what to do, I divinely met a woman who was restored and back with her husband. When we sat down to talk and she began sharing some of the principles in *How God Will Restore Your Marriage* all I could say to her was cry because I'd done everything wrong! I just did not know!! The restored woman (I'm embarrassed because I don't remember what she said her name was) gave me a book from the backseat of her car and told me to take it home and "study" it.

I have to say, the more I read and studied it, I learned so much more but the more I cried and repented to God because I never realized how little I knew about what the Bible said!! Though I could have become even more deeply depressed I chose to become enthusiastic instead, knowing now about God's ability to turn things around in my marriage just as He had in the sweet woman's restored marriage.

The following week, there were many more tears when I ran into the same woman (she must think all I do is cry). But this time I had tears of joy as I ran towards her! I had to tell her that everything had completely turned around with my husband. My husband said that because of the changes he had seen in ME in the two weeks after I got the book, he knew that our marriage was going to work out. He told me that very day he had dropped the divorce for our final hearing!!!!! Talk about discovering the truth just in time. Crying my eyes out (when he told me) I looked down at my husband's hand and saw that he was also wearing his wedding ring!!!! He's never worn his wedding ring since the day of our wedding!!!!

The contentious woman I used to be was gone. It's been three years since I buried her in the truth. The gentle and quiet woman a man longs to have, a wife who is submissive instead of bossy is a person any man would want to stay married and faithful to. Thank you all for the work you're doing so save marriages by writing this *Restore Your Marriage* book. May God bless you!!!

~Jan in New Hampshire, RESTORED

"The OW TOTALLY Out of the Picture!"

We received an email that said,

Good morning RMI. I'm hoping you can help me. I'm the mother of many children that I'd been a homeschooling mom and I heard Erin Thiele speak at a conference last year and was hoping to get further help. At the conference I bought your book *How God Will Restore Your Marriage* book and have read it numerous times. My situations if a very very painful situation. My husband has been committing adultery for years, but it's gotten much worse. He's forced me back to work, putting our children in school, which only increased his unfaithfulness to me. Now he's involved with another woman, a woman whom I worked with. One night a few weeks ago my husband and the other woman came into where I worked, sat passionately together, and even kissed right in front of me! Others I work with saw it too.

As the book says, I remained quiet and said nothing to him. Then things got worse when my husband couldn't find an apartment for himself and his girlfriend, so he came home one night when he was very drunk and demanded that I pack and leave and take the children so the two of them could live in our home. I had simply become so weary that I began to think this might be for the best. But the Lord faithfully revealed the truth to me in time. When I realized that this was surely a trap and scheme of the enemy, the children and I knelt down and began to pray to be able to stay in our homes, ending by singing praises to the God Almighty! That night my husband came home (it was actually 4 in the morning) and said that he didn't want me (us) to go. Is there anything more I should do?

We wrote Cindi back with just a few words of encouragement, "Cindi, just continue to believe and trust God. Listen to His leading you" and also felt led to send her both the Wise Woman and Wise Man. Then we explained she should study the A Wise Woman but the A Wise Man was for her to pray over, but not to show or give it to her husband. We asked her, instead, to put it in a safe place out of sight.

Within a week's time, we received another letter.

Thank you RMI, I have received my miracle!!! My husband is now home with us and the other woman is totally out of the picture!!! Praise You LORD. And this isn't the end of my praise. One day I went into our bedroom and I saw the WM Men's Manual lying open on his side of the bed!! I had NO idea how he'd found it. The most amazing part is that my husband is not even a reader! Praise the Lord for His faithfulness!! Blessings to all of you for what you're doing to save families!

~Cindi in Pennsylvania, RESTORED

"EH Girlfriend Moved Out!"

Another letter we received was from Brenda in northern Alabama. She was asking us to send the book, *How God Will Restore Your Marriage* for her daughter who she said had a marriage that was in trouble. When we followed up a week later to make sure she received the book, this was what the next letter said we got four months later:

Thank you all for what you've done!! I'm so excited to hear from you. I'm sorry I didn't write back sooner. I am so thrilled to tell you know that my daughter received a phone call from her mother-in-law telling her that her husband's "girlfriend" had just moved out of her husband's apartment. Then the very next day my daughter moved back in! This is nothing short of a miracle and it's due to all of you. No words can express how I am feeling at this moment.

~Brenda in Alabama, is RESTORED

Chapter 48

Gloria

"A broken and a contrite heart,
O God, You will not despise."

— Psalm 51:17

"My Parent's are Restored!!!"

Dear Restore Ministries International, I have been coming to your website for many years. I purchased every book you offer. My marriage was never in trouble, I came looking for hope because my mom and dad have been divorced for years but I just believed that somehow and in some way I could help them get back together. Today I am writing to say that that my parents just REMARRIED last week! Hallelujah!! Praise You Lord Jesus!!!

What should have been my parent's 50th anniversary is the day my father asked my mother to remarry him and she said YES!! It's only then that my mother confessed to my dad that she knew someday they'd be together again. My mom and I studied a A *Wise Woman* and I have to say that even though it restored my parents, the other miracle is about the changes it made in me! You need to know that I was horribly contentions towards everyone and I never once let my husband finish a sentence before I'd correct him and set him straight. I never thought it was horrible because everyone of my friends acts the same way towards their husbands, so I thought it was the way a wife was supposed to be. Then I started watching their marriages fall apart, husband divorcing my friends and often it was my girlfriends who'd file. But I just thought it's normal. But when I experienced what my parents' divorce did to me and my brothers I just didn't want the same for my kids. So by me helping my mom (and dad) I believe my marriage and life are now built on the Rock and I no longer am tearing my house down with my own hands (or actually my mouth and bad attitude).

My mom's faith helped me to believe it would happen. Even though my parents had divorced six years ago so that my dad could marry the woman he met at work, my mom believed once she read *How God Can and Will Restore Your Marriage*.

What's kind of sad is that my dad's second wife just recently died of Alzheimer's. I'd read this verse in my bible, "And I gave her time to repent; and she does not want to repent of her immorality. Behold, I will cast her upon a bed of sickness, and those who commit adultery with her into great tribulation, unless they repent of her deeds" (Revelations 2:21-22) when she'd been diagnosed but never thought she'd pass away and pass so quickly.

What turned my father around was the five long years he watched his second wife suffering. Having to care for her (which I believe was his "great tribulation") actually helped him to draw closer to the Lord. God's Word, his bible, finally became something meaningful to him. God is faithful! Thank You Lord!

So you see, RMI and Erin, you saved an entire family from destruction. There are no words to express my entire family's gratitude. All I can say Thank you from the bottom of my heart!!!

~Gloria's parents in Georgia, RESTORED

As this book got larger and larger we were unable to keep up with printing all of them in a book!

What you have read is just a *small sample* of the POWER and FAITHFULNESS of God that are told through countless restored marriages! We continue to post new restored marriage, and restored relationship testimonies (children, siblings, parents, etc.) on our site each week.

Don't let ANYONE try to convince you that God cannot restore YOUR marriage! It is a lie. The TRUTH is that He is MORE THAN ABLE!! Is Your Marriage... Crumbling? Hopeless? Or Ended in Divorce?

At Last There's Hope!

Have you been searching for marriage help online? It's not by chance, nor is it by coincidence, that you have this book in your hands. God is leading you to Restore Ministries that began by helping marriages that *appear* hopeless—like yours!

God has heard your cry for help in your marriage struggles and defeats. He predestined this **Divine Appointment** to give you the hope that you so desperately need right now!

We know and understand what you are going through since many of us in our restoration fellowship have a restored marriage and family! No matter what others have told you, your marriage is not hopeless! We know, after filling almost two books of restored marriage testimonies, that God is able to restore any marriage—especially yours!

"Behold, I am the LORD, the God of all flesh; is anything too difficult for Me?" (Jeremiah 32:27).

If you have been told that your marriage is hopeless or that without your husband's help your marriage cannot be restored! Each week we post a new Restored Relationship from one of our Restoration Fellowship Members that we post on our site.

"Ah Lord GOD! Behold, You have made the heavens and the earth by Your great power and by Your outstretched arm! Nothing is too difficult for You"! (Jeremiah 32:17).

If you have been crying out to God for more help, someone who understands, someone you can talk to, then we invite you to join our RMI Restoration Fellowship. Since beginning this fellowship, we have seen more marriages restored on a regular basis than we ever thought possible!

Restoration Fellowship

Restoration is a "narrow road"—look around, most marriages end in divorce! But if your desire is for a restored marriage, then our Restoration Fellowship is designed especially for you!

Since beginning this fellowship, we have seen marriages restored more consistently than we ever thought possible.

Let us help you stay committed to "working with God" to restore your marriages. Restoration Fellowship can offer you the help, guidance, and support you will need to stay on the path that leads to victory—*your* marriage restored!

Let us assure you that all of our marriages were restored by GOD (through His Word) as we sought Him to lead us, teach us, guide us and transform us through His Holy Spirit. This, too, is all *you* need for *your* marriage to be restored.

However, God continues to lead people to our ministry and fellowship to gain the faith, support and help that so many say that they needed in their time of crisis.

"*I want you to know how MUCH the RMI resources, the fellowship and the website have meant to me. Yes, I will candidly say all you NEED is the Word of God to restore your marriage, but RMI shines a brilliant light on that Word with so much encouragement. I really believe that this would be a much longer more painful journey with a LOT more detours if I had not had the resources of RMI to go back to again and again, leading me to a genuine love for God.*" K.H. in North Carolina

"*My husband did not talk to me for the first six months after he left but God continued His faithfulness to help me not give up; He used Restore*

Ministries to encourage me – I could not have made it without you." Michelle, **Restored** in Wisconsin

"God led me to Restore Ministries, which provided the encouragement I needed at exactly the time I needed it. All of the resources you required for membership helped me. They gave me encouragement, hope and a sense of peace. Stephanie, **Restored** in Kansas

"I cannot thank God enough for His unfailing mercies and for restoring our marriage after five years of marital troubles and separation! I was on the website every day for encouragement. After seeing the changes in me, my husband started to change, he held me and told me he was sorry for all that happened, that that he loved me and always did despite everything!" Lina, **Restored** in Ghana

Join our Restoration Fellowship TODAY and allow us to help YOU **restore** YOUR marriage.

Like What You've Read?
If you've been blessed by this book
By the Word of Their Testimony
(Book 3): Nothing is Impossible With God
Get the WOTT Series available
on EncouragingBookstore.com & Amazon.com

By the Word of Their Testimony (Book 1): Incredible and Powerful Testimonies of Restored Marriages

By the Word of Their Testimony (Book 2): No Weapon Formed Against you will Prosper

Word of Their Testimony (Book 3): Nothing is Impossible With God

Restore Ministries International

POB 830
Ozark, MO 65721
USA

For more help
Please visit one of our Websites:

EncouragingWomen.org

HopeAtLast.com

RestoreMinistries.net

RMIEW.com

RMIOU.com

Aidemaritale.com (French)

AjudaMatrimonial.com (Portuguese)

AyudaMatrimonial.com (Spanish)

EncouragingMen.org

Made in the USA
Middletown, DE
28 February 2023

25828915R00128